Listen and Learn
Russian

BY HELEN MICHAILOFF

Instructor of Russian, Columbia University

and

The Editorial Staff of

DOVER PUBLICATIONS, INC.

DOVER PUBLICATIONS, INC.
NEW YORK

Published in Canada by General Publishing
Company, Ltd., 30 Lesmill Road, Don Mills,
Toronto, Ontario.

Published in the United Kingdom by Con-
stable and Company, Ltd., 10 Orange Street,
London WC 2.

International Standard Book Number:
0-486-20879-6

Manufactured in the United States of America
Dover Publications, Inc.
180 Varick Street
New York, N.Y. 10014

CONTENTS

4   CONTENTS

SIDE FOUR

APPENDICES
(not recorded)

INTRODUCTION

The Plan and Presentation of "Listen and Learn"

Listen and Learn Russian is designed to give you the basic sentences, phrases, and vocabulary that you will need in almost every travel situation. It does not attempt to teach the grammatical structure of Russian through a series of graded lessons. You will, however, absorb much of the structure of Russian in the same unconscious way in which you first learned English as a child. You need not start at the beginning; listen and learn whatever sections interest you. Although a systematic study is probably most desirable, don't feel obliged to master any one series of phrases before going on to the next. This course differs from many others in that whatever you learn will be useful, regardless of the amount of previous study or your ability to remember.

You will observe that *Listen and Learn Russian* is a straightforward course, designed to help you solve real travel problems. Its value rests as much on what is omitted as on what is included. You will find the phrase "May I have some small change?" (an urgent need in travel), but do not expect to find a sentence like "This is my brother's coat."

Listen and Learn Russian teaches you principally what *you* will say. This plan is a deliberate editorial policy based on travel experience. No editor could possibly anticipate the exact form in which your questions will be answered. A waiter may be anything from taciturn to over-talkative, and may answer your question with a silent nod or with questions about life in the United States. The editors have therefore framed most of the questions and statements in order to elicit a simple response that will probably contain the very words of your question.

The section on making yourself understood (entries 67 to 81) will also aid you in understanding others. Phrases such as "Please speak more slowly" and "Repeat it, please" are essential because the correct pronunciation you will achieve through imitation will often suggest to the listener a greater mastery of the language than you may actually have.

Suggested Method for Study—The Records

In the recordings, each item is spoken in English and in Russian, followed by a pause sufficiently long to allow for repetition.* If you are completely unfamiliar with Russian, the pause may seem short at first, but you will find that as you become more familiar with each phrase the pause will be adequate for repetition.

In the beginning sections of the records the Russian is spoken slowly and deliberately so that you can more easily grasp and assimilate the language sounds. In later sections, the tempo becomes more normally rapid. Until you become accustomed to the sounds of the language, you might best concentrate on the slower sections. Bear in mind that the slower pace is presented for teaching purposes but that Russian like all languages is spoken rapidly at a rate comparable to the later sections of the recording and the conversation dialogues. After some practice, you may wish to use

---

* Except for three brief sections of dialogue delivered at the normal rate of speech in order to acquaint you with the rhythm and flow of Russian in ordinary conversation. In the recordings, each such section begins with a reminder that dialogue follows.

the pause to anticipate the next item and check your pronunciation against that of the speaker. If at first you listen to the records while following the text, you will find the separate study of the record and manual more meaningful. Play the records whenever you have an opportunity, while working, engaging in a hobby—whenever you are within listening distance of a record player. Although active participation is best, even passive but repeated listening will familiarize you with useful Russian.

If you have a tape recorder available, we recommend that you record sections of the *Listen and Learn* record along with your own repetition in the pause. Critical, objective listening to the playback will enable you to compare and improve your pronunciation.

Suggested Method for Study—The Manual

The *Listen and Learn Russian* manual is complete in itself and is designed so that you can carry it in your pocket for reference and study. Read it at odd moments—while commuting, eating, waiting—and try to learn 10 or 15 phrases a day, testing your pronunciation against that of the records when you have an opportunity. In 30 to 60 days, depending upon your rate of study, you will know what is essential for travel.

Be sure to take the manual with you when you go abroad. All that you have learned will be available to you for reference and refresher study. You will find the extensive topic and word index on pages 180–192 especially helpful. Notice that each entry in the book is numbered and that the index refers to these numbers. This enables you to locate the information you need quickly, without having to search the entire page.

Use the index to test yourself. It contains every

important word and phrase that you have learned in *Listen and Learn Russian.* Test your vocabulary and your ability to form phrases and questions from the words in the index.

The manual is designed to help you form additional sentences of your own. For the words in square brackets you can substitute the words immediately following (in the indented entries below). For example, the entry.

> I am [a student].
> —— a teacher.
> —— a businessman.
> —— an engineer.

provides four sentences: "I am a student," "I am a teacher," "I am a businessman," and "I am an engineer." As your Russian vocabulary increases, you will find that you can express a wide range of thoughts by the proper substitution of words in these model sentences. Feminine forms of nouns and adjectives are enclosed in parentheses and marked *f*. These alternative forms are not recorded.

Speak Russian When You Travel

When you travel in Russia, do not be timid about using what you have learned. The native listener is always pleased and flattered when you attempt to speak his language. Whether this is your first trip or your twenty-first, your native listener will know that you are an American (years of intensive study will never disguise this fact), and he is ready to accept pronunciation and grammar that is less than perfect. So do not be self-conscious if your speech is halting and awkward. Speak politely, boldly, and clearly. Timid mumbling may be a greater barrier to comprehension than faulty palatals. Remember that your purpose is to communicate, not to pass as a native Russian.

Listen and Learn Russian will enable you to communicate on a simple but very practical level. You will make yourself understood on everyday matters. With time and practice, improvement will come and the range of your conversation will expand. Do not, however, let your present inability to discuss Russian music or current affairs inhibit you in asking questions in Russian. You know your own language limitations, and you must speak Russian within and in spite of them.

Bear in mind that your Russian listener is not judging or grading you. He is kindly disposed towards you and is especially interested in trying to communicate. When you succeed in making yourself understood in Russian, you will have achieved your aim. If you are interested in a grade, score yourself 100%.

Speak the Russian you have learned in *Listen and Learn Russian*. The effort will not only make your travel more exciting and rewarding, but will also contribute to better foreign relations. Many Americans go abroad expecting all peoples of the world to speak English—an attitude that non-Americans find narrow. If you are willing to meet and speak with people in their own language, you may not impress them with your command of the subjunctive, but you will create an impression more representative of the warmth and democratic spirit of America. This impression may be more valuable than thousands of words of propaganda.

FOR FURTHER STUDY

After you have mastered the material of *Listen and Learn Russian,* you may wish to continue with formal study in order to become more fluent in speaking, reading, and writing. It is entirely possible to carry on study by yourself with a few well-chosen books and with such audio-visual aids as movies and broadcasts.

The following books can be purchased through your local dealers at the publisher's current (1983) list price:

Dictionaries

New English-Russian and Russian-English Dictionary by M. A. O'Brien. Dover Publications, Inc., 180 Varick Street, New York, NY 10014. $7.50.

Russian-English Dictionary, edited by A. I. Smirnitsky. E. P. Dutton & Co., Inc., 201 Park Ave. S., New York, NY 10003. $24.75.

Grammars

Penguin Russian Course, by J. L. Fennel. Penguin Books, Inc., 625 Madison Ave., New York, NY 10022. $4.95.

Introductory Russian Grammar, by Galina Stilman, et al. John Wiley & Sons, Inc., 605 3rd Ave., New York, NY 10158. $21.95.

Essentials of Russian, by A. Von Gronicka and

H. Bates-Yakobson. Prentice-Hall, Inc., Englewood Cliffs, NJ 07632. $19.95.

Readers

Russian Short Stories, edited by John Iwanik. D. C. Heath & Co., 2700 Richardt Ave., Indianapolis, IN 46219. $9.95.

New Voices: Contemporary Soviet Short Stories, edited by K. Harper, et al. Harcourt Brace Jovanovich, Inc., 757 3rd Ave., New York, NY 10017. $11.95.

Contemporary Russian Reader, by Lila Pargment. Frederick Ungar Publishing Co., Inc., 250 Park Ave. S., New York, NY 10017. $8.50.

General Literature

Your local dealer or college book store probably has only a small selection of foreign language books, but a visit there may be rewarding. The following specialist dealers have larger stocks ranging from elementary to advanced levels. Some will send you catalogs and announcements if you drop them a card.

Barnes and Noble, Inc., 105 Fifth Ave., New York, NY 10003.

Four Continent Book Corp., 149 Fifth Ave., New York, NY 10010.

Kroch's and Brentano's, 29 South Wabash Ave., Chicago, IL 60603.

R. H. Macy's Book Department, Herald Square, New York, NY 10001.

Schoenhof's Foreign Books, Inc., 1280 Massachusetts Ave., Cambridge, MA 02138.

Universal Book Store, 5458 N. 5th St., Philadelphia, PA 19120.

Znanie Book Store, 5237 Geary Blvd., San Francisco, CA 94118.

Rizzoli International Book Store, 712 Fifth Ave., New York, NY 10019.

Newspapers and Periodicals

A good selection of Russian magazines and newspapers is available at the Four Continent Book Corp. Single copies of *Pravda* and *Izvestiya* may be obtained at some newsstands in the Times Square area of New York City, and in major cities throughout the country. *Novoye russkoye slovo* is published and distributed to some newsstands in New York City or can be obtained from 461 8th Ave., New York.

PRONUNCIATION

The simplified phonetic transcription is given as an aid to correct pronunciation. The transcription should be read as though it were English, with special attention to those sounds which have no exact English equivalents. The phonetic transcription has been devised as a first step in your language study. It cannot replace the effectiveness of imitating a native speaker, and it is therefore of utmost importance to use it in conjunction with the records which accompany the course. This will prevent your falling into bad habits of pronunciation. If you are unable at any subsequent time, however, to refer to the records, when actually traveling, for instance, then the transcription will at least help you to recall the correct pronunciation. In our system, consistency is sometimes sacrificed for simplicity and ease of comprehension. You are urged to use the transcription only as a temporary guide. If you study in a class or with a private teacher, you will probably be asked not to use the transcription.

Most beginners greatly over emphasize the task of learning Russian letters. The mastery of their pronunciation in reading is not difficult because there are 33 letters and their pronunciation is reasonably regular. The problem is not akin to learning how to read English with all its spelling and phonetic irregularities. Even if you do not go on to further study, you will be amply repaid for this effort by your ability to read proper names, street signs and notices, and to use Russian dictionaries.

Notes on Vowels

Vowel sounds in Russian as in most foreign languages, usually present the greatest problem, not only to the beginner, but also to the advanced student. The following notes on pronunciation are designed to direct your listening and make your ear more aware of the differences between English and Russian. (But bear in mind that the mastery or study of these differences is not essential to making yourself understood.)

Russian vowels are classed as "hard" and "soft."

Hard		*Soft*	
у	oo	ю	yoo
о	aw	ё	yaw
а	ah	я	yah
э	eh	e	yeh
ы	ih	и	ee

When any of these vowels stands alone or occurs at the beginning of a word, it has the value given above. More important, however, is the effect of a soft vowel on the consonant which precedes it. (The hard vowels are rather similar to their English counterparts.) A consonant before a soft vowel is palatalized, that is, pronounced with the tongue flat against the palate rather than in the normal position. This has the effect of introducing a short *y*, as in *yes*, after the consonant. For example, a soft *t* resembles the *t* of *tune* (tyoon, not toon); a soft *d* resembles the *d* of *duty* (DYOO-tee, not DOO-tee), a soft *n* is like the *n* of *canyon*, etc. Note the following examples:

тётя	(aunt)	TYAW-tyah
делать	(to do)	DYEH-laht^y
нет	(no)	nyet
место	(place)	MYES-tuh

The consonants ш (sh), щ (schch), ц (ts), ч (ch), and ж (zh) do not change, and a soft vowel following any of these is pronounced like its hard counterpart.

In addition to the effect which hard and soft vowels have on consonants preceding them, it should be pointed out that, as in English, Russian vowels have their full value only in stressed syllables where they are pronounced strongly and clearly. In unstressed syllables, they are slurred, shorter in duration, and they undergo slight changes in quality. An example of this change can be seen in words like in*f*orm and in*f*ormation, sena*t*or and sena*t*orial. No phonetic transcription can indicate these changes precisely, but in general, the following remarks apply to those vowels which are the most variable.

o　In a stressed syllable, *aw* as in l*aw*.
　　In the syllable immediately preceding the stressed syllable, *ah* as in f*a*ther.
　　Everywhere else, *uh* as in th*e* boy.

a　In a stressed syllable or the one immediately before it, *ah* as in f*a*ther.
　　Everywhere else, somewhat like *uh*, as in th*e* boy.

e　In a stressed syllable, *yeh* as in *y*et.
　　Everywhere else, rather like the *ee* in f*ee*, but considerably shorter.

These remarks on change of quality of the vowel sounds apply to the soft counterpart of a (ah) which is я (yah). The vowels у (oo), и (ee) and ы (ih) tend to lose less of their character in unstressed syllables although they are somewhat shorter. The soft counterpart of o (aw) which is ё (yaw) occurs only in stressed syllables and consequently always retains its clarity. When a palatalized consonant is desired, and there is no vowel following it, the soft sign, ь, is used. It has no sound of its own.

Voiced consonants in Russian (as in other Slavic languages and German) are unvoiced at the end of a word or syllable, or when they are followed by an unvoiced consonant. Thus:

b (б) is pronounced	p
d (д)	,,	t
g (г)	,,	k
z (з)	,,	s
zh (ж)	,,	sh
v (в)	,,	f

These remarks on phonetic differences have been introduced with considerable hesitancy lest they hinder the beginner's speaking. Irregularity and inconsistency of pronunciation is especially present in the pronunciation of Russian numbers and in frequently used words such as *please*, пожалуйста, *pah-ZHAH-loos-tah*. But these hints on pronunciation can increase your comprehension of the spoken language and explain what may appear to be inconsistencies as you listen to the records. The complexities of Russian phonetics have been the subject of numerous dissertations. The student who wishes to pursue the subject may consult: Boyanus, S. C. *Russian Pronunciation*. 2 vols. Cambridge, 1955. $8.00.

Russian Letters	Our Transcription	Notes
A a	ah	as in father
Б б	b or p	as in bed. p as in speak at the end of a word or syllable.
В в	v or f	as in vat. f as in feel at the end of a word or syllable.
Г г	g or k	as in go.*
Д д	d or t	as in day. t as in stay at the end of a word or syllable.
Е е	ye or yeh	as in yet.
Ё ё	yaw	as in yawn.
Ж ж	zh or sh	like the s in measure. sh as in shall at the end of a word or syllable.
З з	z or s	as in zeal. s as in sit at the end of a word or syllable.
И и	ee	as in meet.
Й й	y	occurs only in diphthongs. See section on diphthongs. p. 22.

* In the genitive endings ero and oro and in two or three other words, the r is pronounced like the English v.

Russian Letters		Our Transcription	Notes
К	к	k	as in sky.
Л	л	l	as in let.
М	м	m	as in map.
Н	н	n	as in no.
О	о	aw, ah, or uh	in stressed syllables, aw as in law; in syllables immediately preceding stress, ah as in father; elsewhere, uh as in the.
П	п	p	as in speak.
Р	р	r	rolled with the tip of the tongue as in Italian, Spanish, etc.
С	с	s	as in set.
Т	т	t	as in stay.
У	у	oo	as in food.
Ф	ф	f	as in feel.
Х	х	kh	as in Bach.
Ц	ц	ts	as in lets.
Ч	ч	ch, sh	as in church.
Ш	ш	sh	as in shall.
Щ	щ	shch	as in fresh cheese.

Russian Letters	Our Transcription	Notes
ъ	—	"hard sign" to indicate the preceding consonant is not palatalized.
ы	ih	somewhat as in milk. There is no English equivalent for this sound. It is a short "i" pronounced at the back of the mouth.
ь	y or ʸ	"soft sign" to indicate that the preceding consonant is palatalized, that is, pronounced with the flat part of the tongue.
Э э	e or eh	as in let.
Ю ю	yoo	like the word *you*.
Я я	yah	as in *yard*.

DIPHTHONGS

The letter, й, does not occur alone, but always follows another vowel with which it forms a diphthong. The following table lists the principal diphthongs and their transcriptions.

Russian Letters	Our Transcription	Notes
ай	ah‿ў	as in l*ie*
ей	yeў	as in *Y*ale
ой	oў	as in b*oy*
уй	oo‿ў	as in ph*ooey*, pronounced as one syllable
ий	ee‿ў	as in s*ee y*et
ый	ih‿ў	No English equivalent. Similar to *y* in ver*y*.

THE RUSSIAN ALPHABET

The Russian (Cyrillic) alphabet is given below with the names of the letters written phonetically. It will be necessary to memorize the alphabet if you wish to use a Russian dictionary, and it will help you remember the pronunciation of the letters.

Ordinary Russian		Italic Russian*		Name of Letter
А	а	*А*	*а*	ah
Б	б	*Б*	*б*	beh
В	в	*В*	*в*	veh
Г	г	*Г*	*г*	geh
Д	д	*Д*	*д*	deh
Е	е	*Е*	*е*	yeh
Ё	ё	*Ё*	*ё*	yaw
Ж	ж	*Ж*	*ж*	zheh
З	з	*З*	*з*	zeh
И	и	*И*	*и*	ee
	й		*й*	ee KRAHT-kuh-yuh (short ee)
К	к	*К*	*к*	kah
Л	л	*Л*	*л*	el
М	м	*М*	*м*	em
Н	н	*Н*	*н*	en
О	о	*О*	*о*	aw
П	п	*П*	*п*	peh
Р	р	*Р*	*р*	ehr
С	с	*С*	*с*	es
Т	т	*Т*	*т*	teh

* Russian handwritten script is based upon the Russian Italic and, except for a few letters, may be described as a connected form of the Italic.

Ordinary Russian		Italic Russian		Name of Letter
У	у	*У*	*у*	oo
Ф	ф	*Ф*	*ф*	ef
Х	х	*Х*	*x*	khah
Ц	ц	*Ц*	*ц*	tseh
Ч	ч	*Ч*	*ч*	cheh
Ш	ш	*Ш*	*ш*	shah
Щ	щ	*Щ*	*щ*	shchah
	ъ		*ъ*	TVYAWR-dih‿ĭ znahk (hard sign)
	ы		*ы*	yeh-REE
	ь		*ь*	MYAHKH-kee‿ĭ znahk (soft sign)
Э	э	*Э*	*э*	eh uh-bah-RAWT-nuh-yeh ("e" backwards)
Ю	ю	*Ю*	*ю*	yoo
Я	я	*Я*	*я*	yah

SIDE ONE—BAND I
SOCIAL CONVERSATION

1. **Good day.   (Good afternoon.)***
   Добрый день.
   DAWB-rih_ў dyen^y.

2. **Good morning.**
   Доброе утро.
   DAWB-ruh-yeh OOT-ruh.

3. **Good evening.**
   Добрый вечер.
   DAWB-rih_ў VYEH-chehr.

4. **Good night.**
   Спокойной ночи.
   spah-KOŸ-nuh_ў NAW-chee.

5. **How do you do!   (Hello!)**
   Здравствуйте!
   ZDRAHST-voo_ў-tyeh.

6. **Good-bye.   (See you later.)**
   До свидания.
   duh-sv^yee-DAHN^y-yah.

7. **Until next time.   (So long.)**
   Пока.
   pah-KAH.

8. **I want to see [Comrade Gvozdev].**
   Я хочу видеть [товарища Гвоздёва].
   yah khah-CHOO V^yEE-dyet^y [tah-VAH-r^yee-shchah gvahz-DYAW-vah].

9. —— **Mr. Chernyshev.**
   господина Чернышова.
   gus-pah-D^yEE-nah chehr-nih-SHAW-vah.

* All expressions in Russian or English enclosed in parentheses are alternates or explanations and are not recorded.

10. —— **Mrs. Popov.**
Госпожу Попову.
gus-pah-ZHOO pah-PAW-voo.

11. **Permit me to introduce you.**
Позвольте вас познакомить.
pahz-VAWL^y-tyeh vahs puz-nah-KAW-m^yeet^y.

12. **This is [Yevgheniy Nikolayevich Shcherbakov].**
Это [Евгений Николаевич Щербаков].
EH-tuh [yev-GYEH-n^yee‿ў n^yee-kuh-LAH-yeh-v^yeech shcher-bah-KAWF].

13. —— **my wife.**
моя жена.
mah-YAH zheh-NAH,

14. —— **my husband.**
мой муж.
moў moosh.

'5. —— **my mother.**
моя мать.
mah-YAH maht^y.

16. —— **my father.**
мой отец.
moў aht-YETS.

17. —— **my daughter.**
моя дочь.
mah-YAH dawch.

18. —— **my son.**
мой сын.
moў sihn.

19. —— **my sister.**
моя сестра.
mah-YAH syest-RAH.

20. —— my brother.
мой брат.
moў braht.

21. —— my child.
мой ребёнок.
moў ryeh-BYAW-nuk.

22. —— my friend.
мой друг.
moў drook.

23. Pleased to meet you.   (*lit.* **Very pleasant**)
Очень приятно.
AW-chen^y pr^yee-YAH-tnuh.

24. How are you?
Как вы поживаете?
kahk vih puh-zhee-VAH-yeh-tyeh?

25. Very well thanks, and you?
Очень хорошо, спасибо, а как вы?
AW-chen^y khuh-rah-SHAW, spah-S^yEE-buh, ah kahk vih?

26. How are things?
Как дела?
kahk dyeh-LAH?

27. All right.
Хорошо.
khuh-rah-SHAW.

28. So, so.
Так себе.
tahk syeh-BYEH.

29. How is your family?
Как ваша семья?
kahk VAH-shah syem^y-YAH?

30. Sit down please.
Садитесь пожалуйста.
sah-D^yEE-tyes^y pah-ZHAH-loo-stah.

31. It was very pleasant.
Было очень приятно.
BIH-luh AW-chen^y pr^yee-YAH-tnuh.

32. Give my regards to your aunt and uncle.
Передайте привет вашим тёте и дяде.
*pyeh-ryeh-DAH͜Ĭ-tyeh   pr^yee-VYET   VAH-sheem
TYAW-tyeh ee DYAH-dyeh.*

33. Come to see us again.
Приходите к нам опять.
pr^yee-khah-D^yEE-tyeh k nahm ah-PYAHT^y.

34. What are you doing tonight?
Что вы делаете сегодня вечером?
*shtaw vih DYEH-lah-yeh-tyeh syeh-VAW-dnyah VYEH-
cheh-rum?*

35. May I call on you again?
Можно придти к вам опять?
MAWZH-nuh pr^yee-T^yEE k vahm ah-PYAHT^y?

36. I like you very much.
Вы мне очень нравитесь.
vih mnyeh AW-chen^y NRAH-v^yee-tyes^y.

37. I love you.
Я вас люблю.
yah vahs lyoob-LYOO.

38. Congratulations.
Поздравляю.
puz-drahv-LYAH-yoo.

39. Happy birthday.
Поздравляю с днём рожденья.
puz-drahv-LYAH-yoo s dnyawm rahzh-DYEN^y-yah.

40. Happy New Year.
Счастливого нового года.
shchah-SL^yEE-vuh-vuh NAW-vuh-vuh GAW-dah.

41. Merry Christmas.
Весёлого рождества.
vyeh-SYAW-luh-vuh ruzh-dyeh-STVAH.

PERSONAL MATTERS

42. What is your name?*
Как ваше имя?
kahk VAH-sheh EE-myah?

43. My name is John.
Моё имя Джон.
mah-YAW EE-myah dzhawn.

44. I am 21 years old.
Мне двадцать один год.
mnyeh DVAH-tset^y *ah-D*^{y}*EEN gawt.*

45. I am an American citizen.
Я американский гражданин *m.* (Я американская гражданка *f.*)
yah ah-myeh-r^y*ee-KAHN-sk*^{y}*ee_ў grahzh-dah-N*^{y}*EEN* m.
(*yah ah-myeh-r*^{y}*ee-KAHN-skah-yah grahzh-DAHN-kah* f.)

46. My mailing address is 920 Broadway, New York.
Мой почтовый адрес Бродвей, номер девятьсот двадцать, Нью Йорк.
moў pah-CHTAW-vih_ў AHD-ryes "Broadway" NAW-myehr dyeh-vyet^y*-SAWT DVAHT-tset*^{y}, *"New York."*

47. I am [a student].
Я [студент *m.* (студентка *f.*)].
yah [stoo-DYENT m. *(stoo-DYENT-kah* f.)].

* In Russian the verb "to be" is omitted in the present tense. Thus, *What is your name?* is translated literally as *What your name?*

48. —— a teacher.
преподаватель *m.* (преподавательница
f.)
pryeh-puh-dah-VAH-tyel^y m. (*pryeh-puh-dah-VAH-tyel^y-n^yee-tsah* f.)

49. —— an engineer.
инженер.
een-zheh-NYEHR.

50. —— a business man.
коммерсант.
kuh-myehr-SAHNT.

51. —— a friend of Robert Brown.
друг *m.* Роберта Брауна.
drook m. *RAW -byehr-tah BROWN-ah.*

52. He works for the Jones Company.
Он работает в компании Джонса.
awn rah-BAW-tah-yet f kahm-PAH-n^yee-yee DZHAWN-sah.

53. I am here [on vacation].
Я здесь [на время каникул].
yah zdyes^y [nah VRYEH-myah kah-N^yEE-kool].

54. —— on business.
по делу.
pah DYEH-loo.

55. I am traveling to Kuibyshev.
Я еду в Куйбышев.
yah YEH-doo f KOO⌣ Y̆-bih-shef.

56. I am [warm].
Мне [тепло].
mnyeh [tyep-LAW].

57. —— cold.
холодно.
KHAW-lud-nuh.

58. —— hot.
жарко.
ZHAHR-kuh.

59. —— thirsty.
хочется пить.
KHAW-cheh-tsah pᵞeetᵞ.

60. —— hungry.
хочется есть.
KHAW-cheh-tsah yestᵞ.

61. I am [busy].
Я [занят *m.* (занята *f.*)].
yah [ZAH-nyaht m. (zah-nyah-TAH f.)].

62. —— tired.
устал *m.* (устала *f.*)
oo-STAHL m. (oo-STAH-lah f.)

63. —— in a hurry.
спешу.
spyeh-SHOO.

64. I am angry.
Я сержусь.
yah syehr-ZHOOSᵞ.

65. We are pleased with everything.
Мы всем довольны.
mih fsyem dah-VAWLᵞ-nih.

66. We did not like it.
Нам не понравилось.
nahm nyeh pah-NRAH-vᵞee-lusᵞ.

SIDE ONE—BAND 2
MAKING YOURSELF UNDERSTOOD

67. Do you speak English?
Вы говорите по-английски?
vih guh-vah-RᵞEE-tyeh puh-ahn-GLᵞEE‿Ĭ-skᵞee?

68. Does anyone here speak English?

Кто-нибудь здесь говорит по-английски?

KTAW-n^yee-boot^y zdyes^y guh-vah-R^yEET puh-ahn-GL^yEE_Ў-skee?

69. I read only English.

Я читаю только по-английски.

yah chee-TAH-yoo TAWL^y-kuh puh-ahn-GL^yEE_Ў-sk^yee.

70. I speak a little Russian.

Я говорю немного по-русски.

yah guh-vah-RYOO nyeh-MNAW-guh pah-ROOS-k^yee.

71. Please speak more slowly.

Пожалуйста, говорите медленнее.

pah-ZHAH-loo-stah, guh-vah-R^yEE-tyeh MYED-lyen-yeh-yeh.

72. I do not understand.

Я не понимаю.

yah nyeh puh-n^yee-MAH-yoo.

73. Do you understand me?

Вы понимаете меня?

vih puh-n^yee-MAH-yeh-tyeh myeh-NYAH?

74. I do not know.

Я не знаю.

yah nyeh ZNAH-yoo.

75. I do not think so.

Я не думаю.

yah nyeh DOO-mah-yoo.

76. Repeat it, please.

Повторите, пожалуйста.

puf-tah-R^yEE-tyeh, pah-ZHAH-loo-stah.

77. Write it down please.

Напишите это, пожалуйста.

nah-p^yee-SHEE-tyeh EH-tuh, pah-ZHAH-loo-stah.

78. What does this word mean?
Что значит это слово?
shtaw ZNAH-cheet EH-tuh SLAW-vuh?

79. What is this (that)?
Что это?
shtaw EH-tuh?

80. How do you say "pen" in Russian?
Как сказать "pen" по-русски?
kahk skah-ZAHTʸ "pen" pah-ROOS-kʸee?

81. How do you spell the word "счёт"?
Как пишется слово "счёт"?
kahk PʸEE-sheh-tsah SLAW-vuh "shchawt"?

GENERAL EXPRESSIONS

82. Yes.
Да.
dah.

83. No.
Нет.
nyet.

84. Perhaps.
Может быть.
MAW-zhet bihtʸ.

85. Please.
Пожалуйста.
pah-ZHAH-loo-stah.

86. Excuse me.
Извините.
eez-vʸee-NʸEE-tyeh.

87. Thanks very much.
Спасибо большое.
spah-SʸEE-buh bahlʸ-SHAW-yeh.

88. You are welcome.
Пожалуйста.
pah-ZHAH-loo-stah.

89. All right.
Хорошо.
khuh-rah-SHAW.

90. Don't mention it.
Не стоит.
nyeh STAW-ʸeet.

91. Very good.
Очень хорошо.
AW-chenʸ khuh-rah-SHAW.

92. It is not important.
Это не важно.
EH-tuh nyeh VAHZH-nuh.

93. Do not bother, please.
Пожалуйста не беспокойтесь.
pah-ZHAH-loo-stah nyeh byes-pah-KOY̆-tyesʸ.

94. Who are you?
Кто вы?
ktaw vih?

95. Who is [that boy]?
Кто [этот мальчик]?
ktaw [EH-tut MAHLʸ-cheek]?

96. —— that young girl.
эта девушка.
EH-tah DYEH-voosh-kah.

97. —— that man.
этот мужчина.
EH-tut moo-SHCHEE-nah.

98. —— that woman.
эта женщина.
EH-tah ZHEN-shchee-nah.

99. Where can I wash my hands?
Где я могу помыть руки?
gdyeh yah mah-GOO pah-MIHT^y ROO-k^{y}ee?

100. Where is [the men's room]?
Где [мужская уборная]?
gdyeh [moosh ·SKAH-yah oo-BAWR-nah-yah]?

101. —— ladies' room.
женская уборная.
ZHEN-skah-yah oo-BAWR-nah-yah.

102. —— bathroom.
ванная комната.
VAHN-nah-yah KAWM-nah-tah.

103. Why?
Почему?
puh-cheh-MOO?

104. How?
Как?
kahk?

105. What do you wish?
Что вы хотите?
shtaw vih khah-T^{y}EE-tyeh?

106. Come here!
Идите сюда!
ee-D^{y}EE-tyeh syoo-DAH!

107. Come in!
Войдите!
vah‿ў-D^{y}EE-tyeh!

108. Wait a moment!
Подождите один момент!
puh-dah-ZHD^{y}EE-tyeh ah-D^{y}EEN mah-MYENT!

109. Not yet.
Нет ещё.
nyet yeh-SHCHAW.

110. Not now.
　　Не теперь.
　　nyeh tyeh-PYEHR^y.

111. Listen!
　　Послушайте!
　　pah-SLOO-shah‿ў-tyeh!

112. Be careful!
　　Осторожно!
　　uh-stah-RAWZH-nuh!

SIDE ONE—BAND 3
DIFFICULTIES AND REPAIRS

113. Can you tell me?
　　Вы можете сказать мне?
　　vih MAW-zheh-tyeh skah-ZAHT^y mnyeh?

114. I am looking for my friends.
　　Я ищу своих друзей.
　　yah ee-SHCHOO svah-^{y}EEKH droo-ZYEЎ.

115. I cannot find my hotel address.
　　Я не могу найти адреса своего отеля.
　　*yah nyeh mah-GOO nah‿ў-T^{y}EE AHD-ryeh-sah
　　svuh-yeh-VAW ah-TEH-lyah.*

116. She lost her handbag.
　　Она потеряла свою сумочку.
　　*ah-NAH puh-tyeh-RYAH-lah svah-YOO SOO-much-
　　koo.*

117. He forgot [his money].*
　　Он забыл [деньги].
　　awn zah-BIHL [DYEN^y-g^{y}ee].

---

　　* Possessive adjectives are not used in Russian as often as in English.

118. —— **his wallet.**
    бумажник.
    boo-MAHZH-nᵞeek.

119. —— **his keys.**
    ключи.
    klyoo-CHEE.

120. **Unfortunately, they missed the train.**
    К несчастью они опоздали на поезд.
    k nyeh-SCHAH-styoo, ah-NᵞEE uh-pahz-DAH-lᵞee nah PAW-yest.

121. **What is the matter?**
    В чём дело?
    f chawm DYEH-luh?

122. **What am I to do?**
    Что мне делать?
    shtaw mnyeh DYEH-lahtᵞ?

123. **My eyeglasses are broken.**
    Мои очки разбились.
    mah-YEE ahch-KᵞEE rahz-BᵞEE-lᵞeesᵞ.

124. **Can you repair these shoes (man's) now?**
    Вы сможете починить эти ботинки при мне?
    vih SMAW-zheh-tyeh puh-chee-NᵞEETᵞ EH-tᵞee bah-TEEN-kᵞee prᵞee mnyeh?

125. **Ask at the lost and found bureau.**
    Обратитесь в бюро потерь и находок.
    uh-brah-TᵞEE-tyesᵞ v byoo-RAW pah-TYEHRᵞ ee nah-KHAW-duk.

126. **The militia station.**
    Участок милиции.
    oo-CHAH-stuk mᵞee-LᵞEE-tsee-ᵞee.

127. **I shall call a militiaman.**
    Я позову милиционера.
    yah puh-zah-VOO mᵞee-lᵞee-tsᵞee-ah-NYEH-rah.

128. The American Consulate.
Американское консульство.
ah-myeh-r^{y}ee-KAHN-skuh-yeh KAWN-sool^y-stvuh.

BAGGAGE

129. Where can we check our baggage through to Kerch? (*lit.* **Where can we give up our baggage for sending to Kerch?**)
Где мы можем сдать вещи в багаж для отправки в Керчь?
gdyeh mih MAW-zhem zdaht^y VYEH-shchee v bah-GAHZH dlyah aht-PRAHF-k^{y}ee f kyerch?

130. I want to leave these packages here for a few hours.
Я хочу оставить здесь эти пакеты на несколько часов.
yah khah-CHOO ah-STAH-v^{y}eet^y zdyes^y EH-t^{y}ee pah-KYEH-tih nah NYEH-skul^y-kuh chah-SAWF.

131. Handle this very carefully.
Обращайтесь с этим очень осторожно.
ah-brah-SHCHAH‿Y̆-tyes^y s EH-t^{y}eem AW-chen^y ah-stuh-RAWZH-nuh.

132. Follow me.
Идите за мной.
ee-D^{y}EE-tyeh zah MNOY̆.

SIDE TWO—BAND I
CUSTOMS

133. Where is the customs office?
Где таможня?
gdyeh tah-MAWZH-nyah?

134. Here is [my baggage].
Вот [мой багаж].
vawt [moў bah-GAHSH].

135. —— my passport.
мой паспорт.
moў PAHS-purt.

136. —— my identification card.
моё удостоверение личности.
mah-YAW oo-duh-stuh-vyeh-RYEH-n^yee-yeh L^yEECH-nuh-st^yee.

137. —— my health certificate.
моё свидетельство о здоровье.
mah-YAW sv^yee-DYEH-tyel^y-stvuh aw zdah-RAW-v^yyeh.

138. —— my visitor's visa.
моя виза туриста.
mah-YAH V^yEE-zah too-R^yEE-stah.

139. I am in transit.
Я еду транзитом.
yah YEH-doo trahn-Z^yEE-tum.

140. The bags over there are mine.
Чемоданы вон там мои.
cheh-mah-DAH-nih vawn tahm mah-YEE.

141. I have nothing to declare.
У меня ничего нет подлежащего пошлине.
oo myeh-NYAH n^yee-cheh-VAW nyet pud-lyeh-ZHAH-shcheh-vuh PAWSH-l^yee-nyeh.

142. All this is for my personal use.
Всё это для моего личного употребления.
vsyaw EH-tuh dlyah muh-yeh-VAW L^yEECH-nuh-vuh oo-puh-tryeb-LYEH-n^yee-yah.

143. Is it necessary to open all the suitcases?
Нужно открыть все чемоданы?
NOOZH-nuh ut-KRIHT^y fsyeh cheh-mah-DAH-nih?

144. I cannot open this trunk.
Я не могу открыть этот сундук.
yah nyeh mah-GOO aht-KRIHT^y EH-tut soon-DOOK.

145. There is nothing here but clothing.
Здесь ничего нет кроме платья.
zdyes^y n^{y}ee-cheh-VAW nyet KRAW-myeh PLAHT^y-yah.

146. These are gifts.
Это подарки.
EH-tuh pah-DAHR-k^{y}ee.

147. Must duty be paid on these things?
Нужно платить пошлину на эти вещи?
NOOZH-nuh plah-T^{y}EET^y PAWSH-l^{y}ee-noo nah EH-t^{y}ee VYEH-shchee?

148. How much must I pay?
Сколько нужно заплатить?
SKAWL^y-kuh NOOZH-nuh zah-plah-T^{y}EET^y?

149. That is all I have.
Это всё, что у меня с собой.
EH-tuh fsyaw shtaw oo myeh-NYAH s sah-BOY̆.

150. Have you finished?
Вы кончили?
vih KAWN-chee-l^{y}ee?

SIDE TWO—BAND 2
TRAVEL DIRECTIONS

151. How do I get [to the airline office]?
Как мне пройти [в контору авиационной линии]?
kahk mnyeh prah‿ў-T^{y}EE [f kahn-TAW-roo ah-v^{y}ee-ah-tsee-AWN-nuh‿ў L^{y}EE-n^{y}ee-^{y}ee]?

152. —— to the ticket reservation office.
в кассу предварительной продажи
билетов.
*ƒ KAHS-soo pryed-vah-RʸEE-tyelʸ-nuh‿y̆
prah-DAH-zhee bʸee-LYEH-tuf.*

153. —— to the Intourist Office.
в контору Интуриста.
ƒ kahn-TAW-roo een-too-RʸEE-stah.

154. How long does it take to go to Archangel?
Сколько часов езды до Архангельска?
*SKAWLʸ-kuh chah-SAWF yez-DIH duh ahr-
KHAHN-gyelʸ-skah?*

155. When will we arrive at Lake Ladoga?
Когда мы прибываем на Ладожское Озеро?
*kahg-DAH mih prʸee-bih-VAH-yem nah LAH-
dush-skuh-yeh AW-zveh-ruh?*

156. Is this the direct way to Sochi?
Это прямой путь в Сочи?
EH-tuh pryah-MOY̆ pootʸ ƒ SAW-chee?

**157. Please show me the way [to the business
section].**
Пожалуйста, покажите мне дорогу [в
деловую часть города].
*pah-ZHAH-loo-stah, puh-kah-ZHEE-tyeh mnyeh dah-
RAW-goo [v dyeh-lah-VOO-yoo chahstʸ GAW-ruh-
dah].*

158. —— to the residential section.
в жилую часть города.
v zhee-LOO-yoo chahstʸ GAW-ruh-dah.

159. —— to the shopping section.
в часть города, где сосредоточены
магазины.
*ƒ chahstʸ GAW-ruh-dah, gdyeh sus-ryeh-dah-
TAW-cheh-nih mah-gah-ZʸEE-nih.*

160. —— **to the city.**
в центр города.
f tsentr GAW-ruh-dah.

161. —— **to the village.**
в деревню.
v dyeh-RYEV-nyoo.

162. —— **out of town.**
загород.
ƵAH-guh-rut.

163. Do I turn [to the north]?
Мне следует повернуть [на север]?
*mnyeh   SLYEH-doo-yet   puh-vyehr-NOOT^y [nah
SYEH-vyehr]?*

164. —— **to the south.**
на юг.
nah yook.

165. —— **to the east.**
на восток.
nah vah-STAWK.

166. —— **to the west.**
на запад.
nah ƵAH-paht.

167. —— **to the right.**
направо.
nah-PRAH-vuh.

168. —— **to the left.**
налево.
nah-LYEH-vuh.

169. What street is this?
Какая это улица?
kah-KAH-yah EH-tuh OO-l^{y}ee-tsah?

170. Where is it?
Где это?
gdyeh EH-tuh?

171. How far is it?
Как далеко это?
kahk dah-lyeh-KAW EH-tuh?

172. Is it near or far?
Это близко или далеко?
EH-tuh BL^{y}EES-kuh EE-l^{y}ee dah-lyeh-KAW?

173. Can I walk there?
Могу я пройти туда пешком?
mah-GOO   yah   prah_ў-T^{y}EE   too-DAH   pyesh-KAWM?

174. Am I going in the right direction?
Я иду в правильном направлении?
yah ee-DOO f PRAH-v^{y}eel^y-num nah-prahv-LYEH-n^{y}ee-^{y}ee?

175. Should I go [this way]?
Нужно мне идти [в эту сторону]?
NOOZH-nah mnyeh ee-T^{y}EE [v EH-too STAW-ruh-noo]?

176. —— that way.
в ту сторону.
f too STAW-ruh-noo.

177. Two streets ahead and then turn left.
Два квартала вперёд и затем свернуть налево.
dvah kvahr-TAH-lah fpyeh-RYAWT ee zah-TYEM svyehr-NOOT^y nah-LYEH-vuh.

178. Is it [on this side of the street]?
Это [на этой стороне улицы]?
EH-tuh [nah EH-tuh_ў stuh-rah-NYEN OO-l^{y}ee-tsih]?

179. —— on the other side of the street.
на другой стороне улицы.
nah droo-GOY̆ stuh-rah-NYEN OO-l^{y}ee-tsih.

180. —— **along the boulevard.**
по бульвару.
pah bool^y-VAH-roo.

181. —— **on the embankment.**
на набережной.
nah NAH-byeh-ryezh-nuh‿ў.

182. —— **across the bridge.**
через мост.
CHEH-ryez mawst.

183. —— **beyond the traffic light.**
за светофором.
zah svyeh-tah-FAW-rum.

184. —— **at the corner.**
на углу.
nah oog-LOO.

185. —— **in the middle.**
посередине.
puh-syeh-ryeh-D^yEE-nyeh.

186. —— **back.**
позади.
puh-zah-D^yEE.

187. —— **straight ahead.**
впереди.
fpyeh-ryeh-D^yEE.

188. —— **inside the station.**
внутри вокзала.
vnoo-TR^yEE vahk-ZAH-lah.

189. —— **outside the station.**
вне вокзала.
vnyeh vahk-ZAH-lah.

190. —— **at the entrance.**
у входа.
oo FKHAW-dah.

191. —— **opposite the park.**
против парка.
PRAW-t^yeef PAHR-kah.

192. —— **beside the school.**
рядом со школой.
RYAH-dum saw SHKAW-luh‿y̆.

193. —— **in front of the monument.**
перед памятником.
PYEH-ryet PAH-myaht-n^yee-kum.

194. —— **in the rear of the store.**
в глубине магазина.
v gloo-b^yee-NYEH·mah-gah-Z^yEE-nah.

195. —— **behind the building.**
позади здания.
puh-zah-D^yEE ZDAH-n^yee-yah.

196. —— **down the stairs.**
вниз по лестнице.
vn^yees pah LYEST-n^yee-tseh.

197. —— **up the hill.** (*lit.* **on the mountain**)
на горе.
nah gah-RYEH.

198. **I am much obliged to you.**
Я вам очень обязан *m.* (обязана *f.*)
yah vahm AW-chen^y ah-BYAH-zahn m. (*ah-BYAH-zah-nah* f.)

SIDE TWO—BAND 3
TICKETS

199. **Where is [the ticket window]?**
Где [билетная касса]?
gdyeh [b^yee-LYET-nah-yah KAHS-sah]?

200. —— **the reservation window?**
      касса предварительной продажи биле-
      тов?
      *KAHS-sah pryed-vah-R^{y}EE-tyel^y-nuh‿ў prah-
      DAH-zhee b^{y}ee-LYEH-tuf?*

**201. How much is [a round trip ticket] to Ki-
slovodsk?**
      Сколько стоит билет [туда и обратно] до
      Кисловодска?
      *SKAWL^y-kuh STAW-^{y}eet b^{y}ee-LYET [too-DAH ee
      ahb-RAHT-nuh] dah k^{y}ees-lah-VAWT-skah?*

202. —— **a one-way ticket.**
      в один конец.
      v ah-D^{y}EEN kah-NYETS.

203. —— **a reserved seat ticket.**
      Плацкарта.
      plahts-KAHR-tah.

204. I have a reservation for this seat.*
      У меня плацкарта на это место.
      *oo myeh-NYAH plahts-KAHR-tah nah EH-tuh
      MYES-tuh.*

205. May I stop at Yessentuki on the way?
      Могу я прервать поездку в Ессентуках?
      *mah-GOO yah pryeh-RVAHT^y pah-YEST-koo v
      yes-syen-too-KAHKH?*

206. Can I get something to eat during the trip?
      Смогу я получить что-нибудь поесть по
      дороге?
      *smah-GOO yah puh-loo-CHEET^y shtaw-n^{y}ee-BOOT^y
      pah-YEST^y pah dah-RAW-gyeh?*

---

* The verb "to have" is not literally translated into Russian.
Possession is expressed idiomatically: у меня ключ *oo myeh-NYAH
klyooch,* "on me key"; у вас ключ *oo vahs klyooch,* "on you key";
etc.

207. First class.
Первый класс.
PYEHR-vih⌣ў klahs.

208. Second class.
Второй класс.
ftah-ROЎ klahs.

209. Third class.
Третий класс.
TRYEH-tᵞee⌣ў klahs.

210. Local train.
Пригородный поезд.
PRᵞEE-guh-rud-nih⌣ў PAW-yest.

211. Express train.
Экспресс.
eks-PRES.

BOAT

212. When must we go on board?
Когда мы должны быть на пароходе?
kahg-DAH mih dahl-ZHNIH bihtᵞ nah pah-rah-KHAW-dyeh?

213. Bon Voyage!
Счастливого пути!
schah-STLᵞEE-vuh-vuh poo-TᵞEE!

214. Where is [the steward]?
Где [официант]?
gdyeh [uh-fᵞee-tsᵞee-AHNT]?

215. —— the cabin steward.
каютный.
kah-YOOT-nih⌣ў.

216. —— the purser.
кассир.
kah-SᵞEER.

217. —— the captain.
капитан.
kah-p^{y}ee-TAHN.

218. The dock.
Док.
dawk.

219. Cabin.
Каюта.
kah-YOO-tah.

220. The deck.
Палуба.
PAH-loo-bah.

221. The deck chair.
Раскладной стул.
rahs-klahd-NOY̆ stool.

AIRPLANE

222. I want [to make a plane reservation].
Я хочу [заказать место на аэроплане].
yah khah-CHOO [zah-kah-ZAHT^y MYES-tuh nah ah-eh-rah-PLAH-nyeh].

223. —— to confirm a plane reservation.
подтвердить свой заказ на место.
put-tvyehr-D^{y}EET^y svoy̆ zah-KAHZ nah MYES-tuh.

224. Is there bus service between the hotel and the airport?
Есть ли автобусное сообщение между отелем и аэропортом?
yest^y l^{y}ee ahf-TAW-boos-nuh-yeh suh-ahp-SHCHEH-n^{y}ee-yeh myezh-DOO ah-TYEH-lyem ee ah-eh-rah-PAWR-tum?

225. At what time will they call for me?
В котором часу за мной заедут?
f kah-TAW-rum chah-SOO zah mnoў zah-YEH-doot?

226. Is flight twenty-three on time?
Полёт номер двадцать три не опаздывает?
pah-LYAWT NAW-myehr DVAH-tsetʸ trʸee nyeh uh-pahz-DIH-vah-yet?

227. How many kilos may I take?
Сколько кило можно взять с собой?
SKAWLʸ-kuh kʸee-LAW MAWZH-nuh vzyahtʸ s sah-BOY̆?

228. How much do they charge per kilo for excess?
Сколько берут за кило сверх нормы?
SKAWLʸ-kuh byeh-ROOT zah kʸee-LAW svyerkh NAWR-mih?

TRAIN

229. Where is the railroad station?
Где вокзал?
gdyeh vahk-ZAHL?

230. When does the train for Dniepropetrovsk leave?
Когда отходит поезд в Днепропетровск?
kahg-DAH aht-KHAW-dʸeet PAW-yest v dnyeh-pruh-pyeh-TRAWVSK?

231. From what track does the train leave?
С какой платформы отходит поезд?
s kah-KOY̆ plaht-FAWR-mih aht-KHAW-dʸeet PAW-yest?

232. Please open the window.
Пожалуйста откройте окно.
pah-zhah-LOO-stah aht-KROЎ-tyeh ahk-NAW.

233. Close the door.
Закройте дверь.
zah-KROЎ-tyeh dvyehrʸ.

234. Where is [the diner]?
Где [вагон-ресторан]?
gdyeh [vah-GAWN-ryeh-stah-RAHN]?

235. —— the sleeper.
спальный вагон.
SPAHLʸ-nih ̮ў vah-GAWN.

236. —— the smoking car.
вагон для курящих.
vah-GAWN dlyah koo-RYAH-shcheekh.

237. Where are we now?
Где мы теперь?
gdyeh mih tyeh-PYEHRʸ?

238. Is smoking permitted here?
Можно здесь курить?
MAWZH-nuh zdyesʸ koo-RʸEETʸ?

BUS, STREETCAR AND SUBWAY

239. What streetcar goes to the Park of Culture and Rest?
Какой трамвай идёт в Парк Культуры и Отдыха?
kah-KOЎ trahm-VAH ̮Ў ee-DYAWT f pahrk koolʸ-TOO-rih ee AWT-dih-khah?

240. Where is the bus stop?
Где остановка автобуса?
gdyeh us-tah-NAWF-kah ahf-TAW-boo-sah?

241. **Can I take this subway line to the University?**

Можно доехать до университета по этой линии метро?

MAWZH-nuh dah-YEH-khaht^y daw oo-n^yee-vyehr-s^yee-TYEH-tah pah EH-tuh ̮ ̌y L^yEE-n^yee-^yee myeh-TRAW?

242. **Do I have to change?**

Нужно пересаживаться?

NOOZH-nuh pyeh-ryeh-SAH-zhee-vah-tsah?

243. **A transfer, please.**

Билет с пересадкой, пожалуйста.

b^yee-LYET s pyeh-ryeh-SAHT-kuh ̮ ̌y, pah-ZHAH-loo-stah.

244. **Conductor, please tell me where I must get off.**

Кондуктор, пожалуйста скажите, где мне сойти.

kahn-DOOK-tur, pah-ZHAH-loo-stah skah-ZHEE-tyeh, gdyeh mnyeh sah ̮ ̌y-T^yEE.

SIDE THREE—BAND 1
TAXI

245. **Please call a taxi for me.**

Пожалуйста вызовите мне такси.

pah-ZHAH-loo-stah VIH-zuh-v^yee-tyeh mnyeh tahk-S^yEE.

246. **Is the taxi free?**

Такси свободно?

tahk-S^yEE svah-BAWD-nuh?

247. **What do you charge [per hour]?**

Сколько вы берёте [за час]?

SKAWL^y-kuh vih byeh-RYAW-tyeh [zah chahs]?

248. —— per kilometer.
за километр.
zah kᵞee-lah-MYEṬR.

249. Please drive [more slowly].
Пожалуйста поезжайте [медленнее].
pah-ZHAH-loo-stah puh-yez-ZHAH_y̆-tyeh [MYED-lyen-nyeh-yeh].

250. —— more carefully.
осторожнее.
uh-stah-RAWZH-nyeh-yeh.

251. Stop here.
Остановитесь здесь.
uh-stah-nah-VᵞEE-tyesᵞ zdyesᵞ.

252. Wait for me.
Подождите меня.
puh-dah-ZHDᵞEE-tyeh myeh-NYAH.

AUTOMOBILE TRAVEL*

253. Where can I rent a car?
Где я могу взять автомобиль на прокат?
gdyeh yah mah-GOO vzyahtᵞ ahf-tuh-mah-BᵞEELᵞ nah prah-KAHT?

254. I have [an international driver's license].
У меня [международное шофёрское свидетельство].
oo myeh-NYAH [myezh-doo-nah-RAWD-nuh-yeh shah-FYAWR-skuh-yeh svᵞee-DYEH-tyelᵞ-stvuh].

255. —— a credit card.
кредитная карточка.
kryeh-DᵞEET-nah-yah KAHR-tuch-kah.

---

* An extensive list (unrecorded) of *Parts of the Car*, *Tools and Accessories*, and *Road Signs* can be found in Appendices IV, V, VI, on pages 147–15❡.

256. A gas station.
Заправочный пункт.
zah-PRAH-vuch-nih‿ў poonkt.

257. A garage.
Гараж.
gah-RAHSH.

258. A mechanic.
Механик.
myeh-KHAH-n^yeek.

259. Is the road [good]?
Дорога [хорошая]?
dah-RAW-guh [khah-RAW-shah-yah]?

260. —— rough.
плохая.
plah-KHAH-yah.

261. Where does that road lead?
Куда ведёт эта дорога?
koo-DAH vyeh-DYAWT EH-tah dah-RAW-gah?

262. What town is this?
Какой это город?
kah-KOY EH-tuh GAW-rut?

263. And the next one?
А следующий?
ah SLYEH-doo-yoo-shchee‿ў?

264. Can you show it to me on the map?
Можете вы показать мне его на карте?
MAW-zheh-tyeh vih puh-kah-ZAHT^y mnyeh yeh-VAW nah KAHR-tyeh?

265. The tank is [empty].
Бак [пустой].
bahk [poo-STOY].

266. —— full.
полный.
PAWL-nih‿ў.

267. Give me forty liters.
Дайте мне сорок литров.
DAH‿Ῐ-tyeh mnyeh SAW-ruk LᶌEET-ruf.

268. Check the oil.
Проверьте масло.
prah-VYEHRᶌ-tyeh MAHS-luh.

269. Put water in the radiator.
Налейте воды в радиатор.
nah-LYEῘ-tyeh vah-DIH v rah-dᶌee-AH-tur.

270. Clean the windshield.
Протрите ветровое стекло.
prah-TRᶌEE-tyeh vyet-rah-VAW-yeh styek-LAW.

271. Lubricate the car.
Смажьте машину.
SMAHSH-tyeh mah-SHEE-noo.

272. Charge the battery.
Зарядите батарею.
zah-ryah-DᶌEE-tyeh bah-tah-RYEH-yoo.

273. Adjust the brakes.
Наладьте тормоза.
nah-LAHTᶌ-tyeh tur-mah-ẔAH.

274. Can you check the tires?
Можете вы проверить шины?
MAW-zheh-tyeh vih prah-VYEH-rᶌeetᶌ SHEE-nih?

275. Can you repair this flat tire now?
Можете вы починить эту сдавшую шину
сейчас же?
*MAW-zheh-tyeh vih puh-chee-NᶌEETᶌ EH-too
SDAHV-shoo-yoo SHEE-noo syeῐ-CHAHS zheh?*

276. The engine overheats.
Мотор перегревается.
mah-TAWR pyeh-ryeh-gryeh-VAH-yeh-tsah.

277. The motor [misses] stalls.
Мотор [даёт перебои] глохнет.
*mah-TAWR [dah-YAWT pyeh-ryeh-BAW-ee]
GLAWKH-nyet.*

278. The windshield wiper does not work.
Стеклоочиститель не работает.
styek-luh-ahchee-ST^yEE-tyel^y nyeh rah-BAW-tah-yet.

279. May I park here for a while?
Можно мне поставить здесь машину на
время?
*MAWZH-nuh mnyeh pah-STAH-v^yeet^y zdyes^y mah-
SHEE-noo nah VRYEH-myah?*

SIDE THREE—BAND 2
HOTEL AND APARTMENT

280. I am looking for [a good hotel].
Я ищу [хороший отель].
yah ee-SHCHOO [khah-RAW-shee‿ǎ ah-TEL^y].

281. —— the best hotel.
самый лучший отель.
SAH-mih‿ǎ LOOCH-shee‿ǎ ah-TEL^y.

282. —— an inexpensive hotel.
недорогую гостиницу.
nyeh-duh-rah-GOO-yoo gah-ST^yEE-n^yee-tsoo.

283. —— a furnished room.
мебелированную комнату.
*myeh-byeh-l^yee-RAW-vahn-noo-yoo KAWM-nah-
too.*

284. I do not want to be in the center of town.
Я не хочу быть в центре города.
*yah nyeh khah-CHOO biht^y f TSEN-tryeh GAW-ruh-
dah.*

285. Where it is not so noisy.
Где не так шумно.
gdyeh nyeh tahk SHOOM-nuh.

286. I have [a hotel reservation].
У меня [заказан номер].
oo myeh-NYAH [zah-KAH-zahn NAW-myehr].

287. Do you have a room free? (*lit.* **rooms**)
У вас есть свободные номера?*
oo vahs yest^y svah-BAWD-nih-yeh nuh-myeh-RAH?

288. Do you have [a single room]? (*lit.* **will you find**)
У вас найдётся [комната]?
oo vahs nah‿ў-DYAW-tsah [KAWM-nah-tah]?

289. —— a double room.
для двоих.
dlyah dvah-^yEEKH.

290. —— a two or three room suite.
двух или трёхкомнатный номер.
dvookh EE-l^yee tryawkh-KAWM-naht-nih‿ў NAW-myehr.

291. Is there a safe deposit box in the hotel?
Есть ли сейф при отеле?
yest^y l^yee s^yeўf pr^yee ah-TYEH-lyeh?

292. I want a room [with a double bed].
Мне нужна комната [с двухспальной кроватью].
mnyeh noozh-NAH KAWM-nah-tah [s dvookh-SPAHL^y-nuh‿ў krah-VAHT^y-yoo].

293. —— with twin beds.
с двумя кроватями.
s dvoo-MYAH krah-VAH-tyah-m^yee.

* номер is used specifically for hotel rooms.

294. —— with a bath.
с ванной.
s VAHN-nuh_y̆.

295. —— with a shower.
с душем.
s DOO-shem.

296. —— with a wash basin.
с умывальником.
s oo-mih-VAHLʸ-nʸee-kum.

297. —— with a balcony.
с балконом.
s bahl-KAW-num.

298. I am looking for a room, [without meals].
Я ищу комнату, [без стола].
yah ee-SHCHOO KAWM-nah-too, [byes stah-LAH].

299. —— for tonight.
на сегодня.
nah syeh-VAW-dnyah.

300. —— for several days.
на несколько дней.
nah NYEH-skawlʸ-kuh dnyey̆.

301. —— for two persons.
для двоих.
dlyah dvah-ʸEEKH.

302. I should like to see the room.
Я хотел бы посмотреть комнату.
yah khah-TYEL bih puh-smah-TRYETʸ KAWM-nah-too.

303. Is it [upstairs]?
Она [наверху]?
ah-NAH [nah-vyehr-KHOO]?

304. —— downstairs.
внизу.
vnʸee-ZOO.

305. Is there an elevator?
Есть ли лифт?
yest^y l^yee l^yeeft?

306. Room service, please.
Бюро обслуживания, пожалуйста.
byoo-RAW ahb-SLOO-zhee-vah-n^yee-yah, pah-ZHAH-loo-stah.

307. Please send a porter to my room at once.
(*lit.* **a man for my luggage**).
Пожалуйста пошлите в мой номер человека за багажом сейчас же.
pah-ZHAH-loo-stah pah-SHL^yEE-tyeh v moy NAW-myehr cheh-lah-VYEH-kah zah bah-gah-ZHAWM syey-CHAHS zheh.

308. —— a chambermaid.
уборщицу.
oo-BAWR-shchee-tsoo.

309. —— a bellhop.
номерного.
nuh-myehr-NAW-vuh.

310. —— a messenger.
посыльного.
pah-SIHL^y-nuh-vuh.

311. Please wake me at a quarter past nine o'clock.
Пожалуйста разбудите меня четверть десятого.
pah-ZHAH-loo-stah rahz-boo-D^yEE-tyeh myeh-NYAH CHET-vyehrt^y dyeh-SYAH-tuh-vuh.

312. Do not disturb me until then.
Не беспокойте меня до тех пор.
nyeh byes-pah-KOY-tyeh myeh-NYAH dah tyekh pawr.

313. We should like to have breakfast in our room.
Мы хотели бы завтракать у себя в номере.
mih khah-TYEH-l^{y}ee-bih ZAHF-trah-kaht^y oo syeh-BYAH v NAW-myeh-ryeh.

314. Who is it?
Кто это?
ktaw EH-tuh?

315. Come back later.
Придите позже.
pr^{y}ee-D^{y}EE-tyeh PAW-zheh.

316. I need [a blanket].
Мне нужно [одеяло].
mnyeh NOOZH-nuh [uh-dyeh-YAH-luh].

317. Bring me [a pillow].
Принесите мне [подушку].
pr^{y}ee-nyeh-S^{y}EE-tyeh mnyeh [pah-DOOSH-koo].

318. —— a pillowcase.
наволочку.
NAH-vuh-luch-koo.

319. —— toilet paper.
бумагу для уборной.
boo-MAH-goo dlyah oo-BAWR-nuh‿y̆.

320. —— sheets.
простыни.
PRAW-stih-n^{y}ee.

321. —— a bath mat.
ванный коврик.
VAHN-nih‿y̆ KAWV-r^{y}eek.

322. —— soap.
мыло.
MIH-luh.

323. —— towels.
полотенца.
puh-lah-TYEN-tsah.

324. —— coat hangers.
вешалки для платья.
VYEH-shahl-k^{y}ee dlyah PLAHT^y-yah.

325. I should like to speak to the manager.
Я хотел *m.* (хотела *f.*) бы поговорить с управляющим.
yah khah-TYEL m. *(khah-TYEH-lah* f.*) bih puh-guh-vah-R^{y}EET^y s oo-prah-VLYAH-yoo-shcheem.*

326. My room key, please.
Ключ от моего номера, пожалуйста.
klyooch ut muh-yeh-VAW NAW-myeh-rah, pah-ZHAH-loo-stah.

327. Are there any letters for me?
Есть ли для меня письма?
yest^y l^{y}ee dlyah myeh-NYAH P^{y}EES^y-mah?

328. What is my room number?
Какой мой номер?
kah-KOЎ moў NAW-myehr?

329. I am leaving at ten o'clock.
Я уезжаю в десять часов.
yah oo-yezh-ZHAH-yoo v DYEH-syet^y chah-SAWF.

330. Please make out my bill as soon as possible.
Пожалуйста приготовьте мой счёт как можно скорее.
pah-ZHAH-loo-stah pr^{y}ee-gah-TAWF^y-tyeh moў shchawt kahk MAWZH-nuh skah-RYEH-yeh.

331. Is the service charge included?
Включено ли обслуживание?
fklyoo-cheh-NAW l^{y}ee ahp-SLOO-zhee-vah-n^{y}ee-yeh?

332. Please forward my mail to American Express in Paris.
Мои письма перешлите, пожалуйста, Американскому Экспрессу в Париж.
mah-YEE PEES^y-mah pyeh-ryeh-SHL^{y}EE-tyeh, pah-ZHAH-loo-stah, ah-myeh-r^{y}ee-KAHN-skuh-moo eks-PREH-soo f pah-R^{y}EESH.

CONVERSATION ON THE TELEPHONE
(At normal rate of speech)

333. Междугороднюю, пожалуйста.
myezh-doo-gah-RAWD-nyoo-yoo, pah-ZHAH-loo-stah.
Long distance, please.

334. Сию минуту.
S^{y}EE-yoo m^{y}ee-NOO-too.
One minute.

335. Алло! Междугородняя? Я хочу говорить с Ленинградом, Кировская подстанция два-семьдесят три-пятьдесят
шесть.
*ahl-LAW! myezh-doo-gah-RAWD-nyah-yah? yah
khah-CHOO guh-vah-R^{y}EET^y s lyeh-n^{y}een-GRAH-
dum, K^{y}EE-ruf-skah-yah paht-STAHN-ts^{y}ee-yah,
dvah-SYEM^y-dyeh-syet tr^{y}ee-pyaht^y-dyeh-SYAHT
shest^y.*
Hello! Long distance? I want to speak with
Leningrad, Kirovskaya, 2-73-56.

336. Ваш номер телефона?
vahsh NAW-myehr tyeh-lyeh-FAW-nah?
Your telephone number?

337. Мой номер Загородная подстанция 4-97-81.
Сколько стоит трёхминутный разговор?
*moÿ NAW-myehr ZAH-guh-rud-nah-yah pahd-
STAHN-ts^{y}ee-yah cheh-TIH-ryeh dyeh-vyeh-NAW-
stuh syem^y, VAW-syem^y-dyeh-syet ah-d^{y}een.
SKAWL^y-kuh STAW-^{y}eet tryawkh m^{y}ee-NOOT-
nih_ÿ rahz-gah-VAWR?*
My number is Zagorodnaya 4-97-81. What is
the charge for a three minute call?

338. Двенадцать рублей шестьдесят пять копеек. Свыше трёх минут — восемь рублей сорок копеек. Соединяю с Ленинградом. Говорите.

dveh-NAH-tsaht^y roob-LYEЎ shest^y-dyeh-SYAHT pyaht^y kah-PYEH-yek. SVIH-sheh tryawkh m^{y}ee-NOOT — VAW-syem^y roob-LYEЎ SAW-ruk kah-PYEH-yek. suh-yeh-dee-NYAH-yoo s lyeh-n^{y}een-GRAH-dum. guh-vah-R^{y}EE-tyeh.

12 rubles 65 kopeks. Over three minutes—8 rubles 40 kopeks. I am connecting you. Speak!

339. Алло! Говорит Глеб Александрович Глинка. Могу я говорить с товарищем Журавлёвым?

ahl-LAW! guh-vah-R^{y}EET glyep ah-lyeh-KSAHN-druh-v eech GLEENK-ah. mah-GOOH yah guh-vah-R^{y}EET^y s tah-VAH-r^{y}ee-shchem zhoo-rahv-LYAW-vihm?

Hello! Gleb Alexandrovich Glinka speaking. May I speak to comrade Zhuravlev?

340. Извините, я вас не слышу. Вас плохо соединили. Говорите, пожалуйста, громче.

eez-v^{y}ee-N^{y}EE-tyeh, yah vahs nyeh SLIH-shoo. vahs PLAW-khuh suh-yeh-d^{y}ee-N^{y}EE-l^{y}ee. guh-vah-R^{y}EE-tyeh, pah-ZHAH-loo-stah GRAWM-cheh.

I am sorry, I can't hear you. The connection is poor. Speak louder, please.

341. Говорит Глеб Александрович Глинка. Я хотел бы поговорить с товарищем Журавлёвым.

guh-vah-R^{y}EET glyep ah-lyeh-KSAHN-druh-v ee ch GLEENK-ah. yah khah-T̄YEL bih puh-guh-vah-R^{y}EET^y s tah-VAH-r^{y}ee-shchem zhoo-rahv-LYAW-vihm.

Gleb Alexandrovich Glinka speaking. I would like to speak to comrade Zhuravlev.

342. Сожалению его нет дома и он вернётся не раньше пол десятого вечера.

suh-zhah-LYEH-nee-yoo yeh-VAW nyet DAW-mah ee awn vyehr-NYAW-tsah nyeh RAHN^y-sheh pawl dyeh-SYAH-tuh-vuh VYEH-cheh-rah.

I am sorry he isn't in and he won't be back until 9.30 this evening.

343. Можете вы передать ему кое-что? Скажите ему, пожалуйста, что звонил Глеб Александрович Глинка. Я буду в Ленинграде в воскресенье. Пусть он позвонит мне в воскресенье утром до двенадцати. Я остановлюсь в отеле "Астория," телефон Центральная 3-45-70, комната № 602.

MAW-zheh-tyeh vih pyeh-ryeh-DAHT^y yeh-MOO KAW-yeh shtaw? skah-ZHEE-tyeh yeh-MOO, pah-ZHAH-loo-stah, shtaw zvah-N^yEEL glyep ah-lyeh-KSAHN-druh-veech GLEENK-ah. yah BOO-doo v lyeh-n^yeen-GRAH-dyeh v vuh-skryeh-SYEN^y-yeh. poost^y awn pah-zvah-N^yEET mnyeh v vuh-skryeh-SYEN^y-yeh OOT-rum daw dvyeh-NAH-tsah-t^yee. yah uh-stah-nahv-LYOO^yS v ah-TYEH-lyeh "ah-STAW-r^yee-yah", tyeh-lyeh-FAWN tsen-TRAHL^y-nah-yah tr^yee SAW-ruk pyaht^y SYEM^y-dyeh-syaht, KAWM-nah-tah NAW-myehr shest^y-SAWT dvah.

Can you give him a message? Please tell him that Gleb Alexandrovich Glinka called. I will be in Leningrad on Sunday. He can telephone me Sunday morning before 12. I shall stay at the Astoria Hotel, telephone Central 3-45-70, room 602.

344. Одну минуту, я запишу.   Отель "Астория," Центральная 3-45-70.   Вы сказали, комната 502?

*ahd-NOO m^{y}ee-NOO-too, yah zah-p^{y}ee-SHOO.   ah-
TYEL^y ah-STAW-r^{y}ee-yah, tsen-TRAHL-nah-yah
tr^{y}ee SAW-ruk pyaht^y SYEM^y-dyeh-syaht. vih skah-
ZAH-l^{y}ee, KAWM-nah-tah pyaht^y-SAWT dvah?*

One minute, I'll write this down.   Hotel Astoria,
Central 3-45-70.   Did you say room 502?

345. Нет, 602.

nyet, shest^y-SAWT dvah.

No, 602.

346. Так. Я записала.   Что-нибудь ещё?

*tahk. yah zah-p^{y}ee-SAH-lah.   SHTAW-n^{y}ee-boot^y
yeh-SHCHAW?*

O.K.   I have written it down.   Anything else?

347. Нет, это всё, благодарю вас.   Извините за
беспокойство.

*nyet, EH-tuh fsyaw, blah-guh-dah-RYOO vahs.
eez-v^{y}ee-N^{y}EE-tyeh zah byes-pah-KOY-stvuh.*

No, that is all, thank you.   Sorry to have
troubled you.

348. Пожалуйста, никакого беспокойства.   Я
передам ему что вы сказали.

*pah-ZHAH-loo-stah, n^{y}ee-kah-KAW-vuh byes-pah-
KOY-stvah.   yah pyeh-ryeh-DAHM yeh-MOO
shtaw vih skah-ZAH-l^{y}ee.*

No trouble at all.   I shall give your message to
him.

349. Большое спасибо.   До свидания.

*bahl^y-SHAW-yeh   spah-S^{y}EE-buh.   duh-sv^{y}ee-
DAHN^y-yah.*

Many thanks.   Goodbye.

350. До свидания.
duh-sv^yee-DAHN^y-yah.
Goodbye.

SIDE THREE—BAND 3
AT THE BAR

351. I should like to have [some vodka].
Я хотел *m.* (хотела *f.*) бы выпить [водки]
yah khah-TYEL m. (*khah-TYEH-lah* f.) *bih VIH-p^yeet^y [VAWT-k^yee].*

352. —— **a cocktail.**
коктейль.
kahk-TYEYL^y.

353. —— **some cognac.**
коньяку.
kuhn^y-yah-KOO.

354. —— **some champagne.**
шампанского.
shahm-PAHN-skuh-vuh.

355. —— **a liqueur.**
ликёру.
l^yee-KYAW-roo.

356. —— **whiskey and soda.**
виски с содой.
V^yEES-k^yee s SAW-duh‿y̆.

357. —— **a glass of sherry.**
рюмку "шерри".
RYOOM-koo SHEHR-r^yee.

358. —— **a mug of beer.**
кружку пива.
KROOSH-koo P^yEE-vah.

359. —— **wine.**
вина.
v^yee-NAH.

360. —— **a bottle of mineral water.**
бутылку минеральной воды.
boo-TIHL-koo   m^yee-nyeh-RAHL^y-nuh ̲ ў   vah-DIH.

361. Let's have another.
Выпьем ещё по одной.
VIH-p^yyem yeh-SHCHAW pah ahd-NOЇ.

362. To your health.
За ваше здоровье.
zah VAH-sheh zdah-RAWV^y-yeh.

SIDE FOUR—BAND I

AT THE RESTAURANT

363. Can you recommend a good restaurant?*
Можете ли вы порекомендовать мне хоро-
ший ресторан?
MAW-zheh-tyeh   l^yee   vih   puh-ryeh-kuh-myen-dah-VAHT^y mnyeh khah-RAW-shee ̲ ў ryes-tah-RAHN?

364. Where can I have [breakfast]?
Где я могу [позавтракать]?
gdyeh yah mah-GOO [pah-ZAHF^L-trah-kaht^y]?

365. —— **lunch.** (*lit.* **a mid-day meal**)
покушать среди дня.
pah-KOO-shaht^y sryeh-D^yEE dnyah.

* Russians are accustomed to having four meals daily.   Breakfast, lunch—eaten informally, dinner served between 4 and 5
o'clock and supper which corresponds to our late dinner.

366. —— **snack.**
перекусить.
*pyeh-ryeh-koo-S*ʸ*EET*ʸ.

367. —— **dinner.**
пообедать.
*puh-ah-BYEH-daht*ʸ.

368. At what time is supper served?
В котором часу подают ужин?
f kah-TAW-rum chah-SOO puh-dah-YOOT OO-zheen?

369. Are you [my waiter]?
Вы [мой официант]?
*vih moў [uh-f*ʸ*ee-tsee-AHNT]?*

370. —— **my waitress.**
моя официантка.
*mah-YAH uh-f*ʸ*ee-tsee-AHNT-kah.*

371. —— **the headwaiter.**
главный официант.
*GLAHV-nih‿ў uh-f*ʸ*ee-tsee-AHNT.*

372. A table for two by the window, if possible.
Столик для двоих у окна, если можно.
*STAW-l*ʸ*eek dlyah dvah-YEEKH oo ahk-NAH, YES-l*ʸ*ee MAWZH-nuh.*

373. Please serve us as quickly as you can.
Пожалуйста подайте нам поскорее.
pah-ZHAH-loo-stah pah-DAH‿Ў-tyeh nahm puh-skah-RYEH-yeh.

374. Bring me [the menu].
Принесите мне [меню].
*pr*ʸ*ee-nyeh-S*ʸ*EE-tyeh mnyeh [myeh-NYOO].*

375. —— **the wine list.**
карту вин.
*KAHR-too v*ʸ*een.*

376. —— **a napkin.**
салфетку.
sahl-FYET-koo.

377. —— **a fork.**
вилку.
V^{y}EEL-koo.

378. —— **a knife.**
нож.
nawsh.

379. —— **a plate.**
тарелку.
tah-RYEL-koo.

380. —— **a teaspoon.**
чайную ложку.
CHAH‿Y̌-noo-yoo LAWSH-koo.

381. —— **a table spoon.**
столовую ложку.
stah-LAW-voo-yoo LAWSH-koo.

382. I want to order something [plain].
Я хочу заказать что-нибудь [простое].
yah khah-CHOO zah-kah-ZAHT^y SHTAW-n^{y}ee-boot^y [prah-STAW-yeh].

383. —— **not too spicy.**
не слишком острое.
nyeh SL^{y}EESH-kum AWST-ruh-yeh.

384. —— **not too sweet.**
не слишком сладкое.
nyeh SL^{y}EESH-kum SLAHT-kuh-yeh.

385. —— **not too fat.**
не слишком жирное.
nyeh SL^{y}EESH-kum ZHEER-nuh-yeh.

386. —— fried.
жареное.
ZHAH-ryeh-nuh-yeh.

387. —— boiled.
варёное.
vah-RYAW-nuh-yeh.

388. I like the meat [rare].
Я люблю мясо [недожареное].
yah lyoob-LYOO MYAH-suh [nyeh-dah-ZHAH-ryeh-nuh-yeh].

389. —— medium.
средней готовности.
SRYED-nʸeў gah-TAWV-nuh-stʸee.

390. —— well done.
хорошо прожареное.
khuh-rah-SHAW prah-ZHAH-ryeh-nuh-yeh.

391. A little more.
Ещё немного.
yeh-SHCHAW nyeh-MNAW-guh.

392. A little less.
Немного меньше.
nyeh-MNAW-guh MYENʸ-sheh.

393. Enough, thank you.
Довольно, спасибо.
dah-VAWLʸ-nuh, spah-SʸEE-buh.

394. This has not been washed clean.
Это не чисто вымыто.
EH-tuh nyeh CHEE-stuh VIH-mih-tuh.

395. This is too cold.
Это слишком холодное.
EH-tuh SLʸEESH-kum khah-LAWD-nuh-yeh.

396. I did not order this.
Я этого не заказывал *m.* (заказывала *f.*)
yah EH-tuh-vuh nyeh zah-KAH-zih-vahl m. (*zah-KAH-zih-vah-lah* f.)

397. Take this away.
Уберите это.
oo-byeh-R^yEE-tyeh EH-tuh.

398. May I change this for a salad?
Можно переменить это на салат?
MAW_ZH-nuh pyeh-ryeh-myeh-N^yEET^y EH-tuh nah sah-LAHT?

399. The bill, please.
Счёт, пожалуйста.
shchawt, pah-_ZHAH-loo-stah.

400. Is the tip included?
Чаевые включены?
chah-yeh-VIH-yeh fklyoo-cheh-NIH?

401. There is a mistake in the bill.
В счёте ошибка.
f SHCHAW-tyeh ah-SHEEP-kah.

402. What is this for?
За что это?
zah shtaw EH-tuh?

403. Keep the change.
Сдачу оставьте себе.
_ZDAH-choo ah-STAHF^y-tyeh syeh-BYEH.

404. The food and service were excellent.
Еда и обслуживание были замечательными.
yeh-DAH ee ahp-SLOO-zhee-vah-n^yee-yeh BIH-l^yee zah-myeh-CHAH-tyel^y-nih-m^yee.

405. Hearty appetite!
Приятного аппетита!
pr^yee-YAHT-nuh-vuh ah-pyeh-T^yEE-tah!

SIDE FOUR—BAND 2

FOOD LIST*

406. Please bring me some water [with ice].

Пожалуйста принесите мне воды [со льдом].

pah-ZHAH-loo-stah pr^yee-nyeh-S^yEE-tyeh mnyeh vah-DIH [sah l^ydawm].

407. —— without ice.

безо льда.

BYEH-zuh l^ydah.

408. Please pass [the bread].

Пожалуйста передайте [хлеб].

pah-ZHAH-loo-stah pyeh-ryeh-DAH⌣Ῐ-tyeh [khlyep].

409. —— the rolls.

булочки.

BOO-luch-k^yee.

410. —— the butter.

масло.

MAHS-luh.

411. —— the sugar.

сахар.

SAH-khahr.

412. —— the salt.

соль.

sawl^y.

413. —— the pepper.

перец.

PYEH-ryets.

* An extensive list (unrecorded) of native food and drink can be found in the *Native Food Supplement*, Appendix I, on pages 118–140.

414. —— **vegetable oil.**
растительное масло.
rah-ST^y*EE-tyel*^y*-nuh-yeh MAHS-luh.*

415. —— **the vinegar.**
уксус.
OOK-soos.

416. —— **the garlic.**
чеснок.
ches-NAWK.

417. —— **the ketchup.**
кетчуп.
kyet-CHOOP.

418. —— **the mustard.**
горчицу.
gahr-CHEE-tsoo.

419. —— **mayonnaise.**
майонез.
mah⌣ў-ah-NEZ.

420. —— **gravy.**
подливку.
pahd-L^y*EEF-koo.*

421. —— **the sauce.**
соус.
SAW-oos.

BREAKFAST FOODS

422. May I have [some fruit juice]? (*lit.* **May I get**)
Могу я получить [какой-нибудь фруктовый
сок]?
mah-GOO   yah   puh-loo-CHEET^y   [*kah-KOЎ-n*^y*ee-*
BOOT^y *frook-TAW-vih⌣ў sawk*]?

423. —— orange juice.
апельсинный сок.
ah-pyel^y-S^yEEN-nih‿ў sawk.

424. —— tomato juice.
томатный сок.
tah-MAHT-nih‿ў sawk.

425. —— stewed prunes.
компот из чернослива.
kahm-PAWT ees chehr-nah-SL^yEE-vah.

426. —— cooked cereal.
какую-нибудь кашу.
kah-KOO-yoo-n^yee-BOOT^y KAH-shoo.

427. —— oatmeal.
овсянку.
ahf-SYAHN-koo.

428. —— toast and jam.
поджареный хлеб и джем.
pahd-ZHAH-ryeh-nih‿ў khlyep ee dzhem.

429. —— honey.
мёд.
myawt.

430. —— an omelet.
омлет.
ahm-LYET.

431. —— soft boiled eggs.
яйца всмятку.
YAH‿Ў-tsah FSMYAHT-koo.

432. —— medium boiled eggs.
яйца вмешочек.
YAH‿Ў-tsah vmyeh-SHAW-chek.

433. —— hard boiled eggs.
яйца вкрутую.
YAH‿Ў-tsah fkroo-TOO-yoo.

434. —— **fried eggs.**
яичницу.
yah-ʸEESH-nʸee-tsoo.

435. —— **scrambled eggs.**
яичницу болтунью.
yah-ʸEESH-nʸee-tsoo bahl-TOONʸ-yoo.

436. —— **bacon and eggs.**
яичницу с грудинкой.
yah-ʸEESH-nʸee-tsoo z groo-DʸEEN-kuh‿y̆.

437. —— **ham and eggs.**
яичницу с ветчиной.
yah-ʸEESH-nʸee-tsoo s vyet-chee-NOY̆.

ENTRÉES

438. I want to order [some chicken soup].
Я хочу заказать [куриный суп].
yah kah-CHOO zah-kah-ZAHTʸ [koo-RʸEE-nih‿y̆ soop].

439. —— **vegetable soup.**
овощной суп.
uh-vahshch-NOY̆ soop.

440. —— **anchovies.**
анчоусы.
ahn-CHAW-oo-sih.

441. —— **beef.**
говядину.
gah-VYAH-dʸee-noo.

442. —— **roast beef.**
ростбиф.
RAWST-bʸeef.

443. —— **roast chicken.**
жареного цыплёнка.
ZHAH-ryeh-nuh-vuh tsihp-LYAWN-kah.

444. —— **duck.**
утку.
OOT-koo.

445. —— **fish.**
рыбу.
RIH-boo.

446. —— **goose.**
гуся.
GOO-syah.

447. —— **lamb.**
баранину.
bah-RAH-n^yee-noo.

448. —— **liver.**
печёнку.
pyeh-CHAWN-koo.

449. —— **lobster.**
омара.
ah-MAH-rah.

450. —— **oysters.**
устриц.
OO-str^yeets.

451. —— **pork.**
свинину.
sv^yee-N^yEE-noo.

452. —— **sardines.**
сардинки.
sahr-D^yEEN-k^yee.

453. —— **sausage.**
колбасу.
kul-bah-SOO.

454. —— **steak.**
бифштекс.
b^yeef-SHTEKS.

455. —— **veal.**
телятину.
tyeh-LYAH-t^yee-noo.

VEGETABLES AND SALADS

456. I want to order [some asparagus].
Я хочу заказать [спаржу].
yah khah-CHOO zah-kah-ZAHT^y [SPAHR-zhoo].

457. —— **beans.**
фасоль.
fah-SAWL^y.

458. —— **cabbage.**
капусту.
kah-POO-stoo.

459. —— **carrots.**
морковь.
mahr-KAWF^y.

460. —— **cauliflower.**
цветную капусту.
tsvyet-NOO-yoo kah-POO-stoo.

461. —— **cucumbers.**
огурцы.
uh-goor-TSIH.

462. —— **lettuce.**
зелёный салат.
zyeh-LYAW-nih‿y sah-LAHT.

463. —— **mushrooms.**
грибы.
gr^yee-BIH.

464. —— **onions.**
лук.
look.

465. —— **green peas.**
зелёный горошек.
zyeh-LYAW-nih‿ў gah-RAW-shek.

466. —— **green peppers.**
зелёный перец.
zyeh-LYAW-nih‿ў PYEH-ryets.

467. —— **boiled potatoes.**
отварной картофель.
ut-vahr-NOŸ kahrᵼTAW-fyelʸ.

468. —— **mashed potatoes.**
картофельное пюре.
kahr-TAW-fyelʸ-nuh-yeh pyoo-RYEH.

469. —— **fried potatoes.**
жареный картофель.
ZHAH-ryeh-nih‿ў kahr-TAW-fyelʸ.

470. —— **rice.**
рис.
rʸees.

471. —— **spinach.**
шпинат.
shpʸee-NAHT.

472. —— **tomatoes.**
помидоры.
puh-mʸee-DAW-rih.

FRUITS

473. Do you have [apples]?
У вас есть [яблоки]?
oo vas yestʸ [YAH-bluh-kʸee]?

474. —— **cherries.**
вишни.
V^y*EESH-n*^y*ee.*

475. —— **grapes.**
виноград.
v^y*ee-nah-GRAHT.*

476. —— **lemons.**
лимоны.
l^y*ee-MAW-nih.*

477. —— **melon.**
дыня.
DIH-nyah.

478. —— **watermelon.**
арбуз.
ahr-BOOS.

479. —— **oranges.**
апельсины.
ah-pyel^y*-S*^y*EE-nih.*

480. —— **peaches.**
персики.
PYEHR-s^y*ee-k*^y*ee.*

481. —— **raspberries.**
малина.
mah-L^y*EE-nah.*

482. —— **strawberries.**
земляника.
zyem-lyah-N^y*EE-kah.*

BEVERAGES

483. I want [a cup of black coffee].
Я хочу [чашку чёрного кофе].
yah khah-CHOO [CHAHSH-koo CHAWR-nuh-vuh
KAW-fyeh].

484. —— coffee with cream.
кофе со сливками.
KAW-fyeh sah SLᵞEEF-kah-mᵞee.

485. —— a glass of milk.
стакан молока.
stah-KAHN muh-lah-KAH.

486. —— tea.
чаю.
CHAH-yoo.

487. —— lemonade.
лимонаду.
lᵞee-mah-NAH-doo.

488. —— soda water with fruit syrup.
газированной воды с сиропом.
gah-zᵞee-RAW-vahn-nuh⌣ ў vah-DIH s sᵞee-RAW-pum.

DESSERTS

489. I want to have [some cake].
Я хочу взять [кусок торта].
yah khah-CHOO vzyahtᵞ [koo-SAWK TAWR-tah].

490. —— a piece of pie.
кусок пирога.
koo-SAWK pᵞee-rah-GAH.

491. —— a small cake.
пирожное.
pᵞee-RAWZH-nuh-yeh.

492. —— cookies.
печенье.
pyeh-CHENᵞ-yeh.

493. —— cheese.
сыру.
SIH-roo.

494. —— **chocolate ice cream.**

шоколадное мороженое.

shuh-kah-LAHD-nuh-yeh mah-RAW-zheh-nuh-yeh.

495. —— **vanilla ice cream.**

сливочное мороженое.

SL^yEE-vuch-nuh-yeh mah-RAW-zheh-nuh-yeh.

SIDE FOUR—BAND 3

CONVERSATION AT THE RESTAURANT
(At normal rate of speech)

496. Желаете вы что-нибудь выпить?

zheh-LAH-yeh-tyeh l^yee vih SHTAW-n^yee-boot^y VIH-p^yeet^y?

Would you like something to drink?

497. Да, принесите нам стопку водки, рюмку "шерри" и бутылку кагора.

dah, pr^yee-nyeh-S^yEE-tyeh nahm STAWP-koo VAWT-k^yee, RYOOM-koo "SHEHR-r^yee" ee boo-TIHL-koo kah-GAW-rah.

Yes, bring us a glass of vodka, a small glass of sherry and a bottle of Kagor.*

498. Что-нибудь на закуску?

SHTAW-n^yee-boot^y nah zah-KOOS-koo?

Any hors d'œuvres?

499. Да, два раза зернистую икру, один раз балык и один раз паштет из печёнки.

dah, dvah RAH-zah zyehr-N^yEE-stoo-yoo eek-ROO, ah-D^yEEN rahz bah-LIHK, ee ah-D^yEEN rahs pahsh-TYET ees pyeh-CHAWN-k^yee.

Yes. Two orders of fresh caviar, one order of cured sturgeon, and one liver paté.

---

* Kagor is a district in the Caucasus—the region in which the wine is produced.

500. Какой суп?

kah-KOЎ soop?

What kind of soup?

501. Бульон с фрикадельками и уху с рыбными ватрушками.

bool^y-YAWN' s fr^{y}ee-kah-D^{y}EL^y-kah-m^{y}ee ee oo-KHOO s RIHB-nih-m^{y}ee vaht-ROOSH-kah-m^{y}ee.

One bouillon with meat balls and one fish soup with fish tarts.

502. Что вы желаете заказать на второе?

shtaw vih zheh-LAH-yeh-tyeh zah-kah-ZAHT^y nah ftah-RAW-yeh?

What would you like to order for the second course?

503. Что вы порекомендуете? Какие блюда особенно хороши у вас?

shtaw vih puh-ryeh-kuh-myen-DOO-yeh-tyeh? kah-K^{y}EE-yeh BLYOO-dah ah-SAW-byen-nuh khuh-rah-SHEE oo vahs?

What would you recommend? What dishes are especially good here?

504. Беф строганов исключительно хорош сегодня. Окуни в сметане тоже хороши.

byef STRAW-gah-nuf ees-klyoo-CHEE-tyel^y-nuh khah-RAWSH syeh-VAW-dnyah. AW-koo-n^{y}ee f smyeh-TAH-nyeh TAW-zheh khuh-rah-SHEE.

Beef Stroganov is exceptionally good today. Perch in sour cream are also good.

505. Мы возьмём один раз беф строганов и один раз отварную стерлядь.

mih vahz^y-MYAWM ah-D^{y}EEN rahz byef STRAW-guh-nuf ee ah-D^{y}EEN rahs ut-vahr-NOO-yoo STYEHR-lyaht^y.

We'll have (*lit.* take) one order of beef Stroganov and one of boiled sturgeon.

506. С каким гарниром?

s kah-K^{y}EEM gahr-N^{y}EE-rum?

And what side dishes?

507. Отварной картофель с зеленью и тушёную
морковь к мясу, а к стерляди подайте
рис и белый соус.

*ut-vahr-NOЎ kahr-TAW-fyel^y z ZYEH-lyen^y-yoo ee
too-SHAW-noo-yoo mahr-KAWF^y k MЎAH-soo, a
k STYEHR-lyah-d^{y}ee pah-DAH‿Ў-tyeh r^{y}ees ee
BYEH-lih‿ў SAW-oos.*

Boiled potatoes and stewed carrots with the meat,
rice and white sauce with the sturgeon.

508. Какой-нибудь салат?

kah-KOЎ-n^{y}ee-boot sah-LAHT?

Any salad?

509. Салат? один зелёный салат; не слишком
много заправки, один сборный салат —
помидоры и огурцы; немного оливко-
вого масла и уксуса, без чеснока,
пожалуйста.

*sah-LAHT? ah-D^{y}EEN zyeh-LYAW-nih‿ў sah-
LAHT, nyeh SL^{y}EESH-kum MNAW-guh zah-
PRAHF-k^{y}ee, ah-D^{y}EEN SBAWR-nih‿ў sah-
LAHT—puh-m^{y}ee-DAW-rih ee uh-goor-TSIH;
nyeh-MNAW-guh ah-L^{y}EEF-kuh-vuh-vuh MAH-
slah ee OOK-soo-sah, byes ches-nah-KAH, pah-
ZHAH-loo-stah.*

Salad? One green salad, not too much dressing;
one mixed salad, tomatoes and cucumbers; a
little olive oil and vinegar, without garlic,
please.

510. Кофе подать вместе с обедом?

*KAW-fyeh pah-DAHT^y VMYEH-styeh s ah-BYEH-
dum?*

Coffee with your dinner?

511. Нет, спасибо. Мы будем пить кофе за десертом.

nyet, spah-S^yEE-buh. mih BOO-dyem p^yeet^y KAW-fyeh zah dyeh-SYEHR-tum.

No, thank you. We'll have coffee with dessert.

512. Хорошо. На десерт у нас шоколадное, сливочное и земляничное мороженое, пирожные, кисель и печёные яблоки.

khuh-rah-SHAW. nah dyeh-SYEHRT oo nahs shuh-kah-LAHD-nuh-yeh, SL^yEE-vuch-nuh-yeh ee zyem-lyah-N^yEECH-nuh-yeh mah-RAW-zheh-nuh-yeh, p^yee-RAWZH-nih-yeh, k^yee-SYEL^y ee pyeh-CHAW-nih-yeh YAHB-luh-k^yee.

Very well.   For dessert we have chocolate, vanilla and strawberry ice cream, cakes, jelly, and baked apples.

513. Один раз шоколадное мороженое, один кисель и набор пирожных. Чашку чёрного кофе, без сливок. Чай с молоком. И, пожалуйста, принесите другой нож. Этот не достаточно острый.

ah-D^yEEN rahs shuh-kah-LAHD-nuh-yeh mah-RAW-zheh-nuh-yeh, ah-D^yEEN k^yee-SYEL^y ee nah-BAWR p^yee-RAWZH-nihkh.   CHAHSH-koo CHAWR-nuh-vuh KAW-fyeh, byez SL^yEE-vuk. chah_ÿ s muh-lah-KAWM. ee, pah-ZHAH-loo-stah, pr^yee-nyeh-S^yEE-tyeh droo-GOÏ NAWSH. EH-tut nyeh dahs-TAH-tuch-nuh AWST-rih_ÿ.

One order of chocolate ice cream, one jelly, and an assortment of cakes.   A cup of black coffee without cream, one tea with milk.   And, please, bring another knife.   This one is not sharp enough.

514. Извините.

eez-v^yee-N^yEE-tyeh.

I am sorry.

515. И, пожалуйста, приготовьте счёт поскорее,
уже поздно и у нас остаётся мало
времени до начала спектакля.

*ee,   pah-ZHAH-loo-stah,   pr^{y}ee-gah-TAWF^y-tyeh
shchawt puh-skah-RYEH-yeh, oo-ZHEN PAWZ-
nuh ee oo nahs uh-stah-YAW-tsah MAH-luh
VRYEH-myeh-n^{y}ee dah nah-CHAH-lah spyek-
TAHK-lyah.*

And please get our bill ready soon, it is late
already, and we have little time before the
beginning of the show.

516. Да, сию минуту.

dah, s^{y}ee-YOO m^{y}ee-NOO-too.

Yes, in a moment.

CONVERSATION AT THE POST OFFICE
(At normal rate of speech)

517. Я хотел бы послать это письмо в Соединённые Штаты. Сколько это будет
стоить?

*yah khah-TYEL bih pah-SLAHT^y EH-tuh p^{y}ees^y-
MAW f suh-yeh-d^{y}ee-NYAWN-nih-yeh SHTAH-
tih.   SKAWL^y-kuh EH-tuh BOO-dyet STAW-
^{y}eet^y?*

I should like to send this letter to the United
States.   How much will the postage cost?

518. Обычной почтой — сорок копеек, воздушной почтой — рубль сорок.

*ah-BIHCH-noў PAWCH-tuh‿ў SAW-ruk kah-
PYEH-yek,   vahz-DOOSH-noў PAWCH-tuh‿ў
roobl^y SAW-ruk.*

By regular mail—40 kopeks, by air mail 1 ruble
40 kopeks.

519. Воздушной почтой, пожалуйста. Дайте
мне шесть марок по десять копеек,
три марки по пятнадцать копеек, и
одну марку за тридцать три копейки.
*vahz-DOOSH-nuh_y̆ PAWCH-tuh_y̆, pah-ZHAH-
loo-stah. DAH_Y̆-tyeh mnyeh shest^y MAH-ruk pah
DYEH-syet^y kah-PȲEH-yek, tr^yee MAHR-kee pah
pyet-NAH-tsaht^y kah-PȲEH-yek, ee ahd-NOO
MAHR-koo zah TR^YEE-tset^y tr^yee kah-PEȲ-k^yee.*
By air mail, please.   Give me 6, ten kopek stamps,
3, fifteen kopek stamps, and a 33 kopek
stamp.

520. Вот ваши марки. Всего два рубля
девяносто восемь копеек. Письмо опу-
стите в почтовый ящик "Письма заграницу."
*vawt VAH-shee MAHR-k^yee. fsyeh-VAW dvah
roob-LYAH dyeh-vyeh-NAW-stuh VAW-syem^y kah-
PYEH-yek. p^yees^y-MAW uh-poo-ST^YEE-tyeh f
pahch-TAW-vih_y̆ YAH-shcheek "PEES^y-mah
zah-grah-N^yEE-tsoo".*
Here are your stamps.   That will be 2 rubles 98
kopeks.   Drop your letter in the mail box
"letters abroad".

521. Благодарю вас. Как я могу послать
посылку в Соединённые Штаты?
*blah-guh-dah-RYOO vahs.   kahk yah mah-GOO pah-
SLAHT^y pah-SIHL-koo f suh-yeh-d^yee-NYAWN-
nih-yeh SHTAH-tih?*
Thank you.   How can I send a package to the
United States?

522. Заполните этот бланк на посылку и сдайте его вместе с посылкой у соседнего окна направо.

zah-PAWL-nʸee-tyeh EH-tut blahnk nah pah-SIHL-koo ee SDAH⌣Ÿ-tyeh yeh-VAW VMЎEH-styeh s pah-SIHL-kuh⌣ў oo sah-SЎED-nyeh-vuh ahk-NAH nah-PRAH-vuh.

Fill out this parcel post form and hand it in together with your package at the next window to the right.

523. Можно застраховать посылку?

MAWZH-nuh zah-strah-khah-VAHTʸ pah-SIHL-koo?

May I insure the package?

524. Да. Укажите сумму страховки в бланке. Что в посылке?

dah. oo-kah-ZHEE-tyeh SOOM-moo strah-KHAWF-kʸee v BLAHN-kyeh. shtaw f pah-SIHL-kyeh?

Yes. You indicate the amount of insurance on the form. What does the package contain?

525. Только грелка на чайник. Ничего бьющегося.

TAWLʸ-kuh GRYEL-kah nah CHAH⌣Ÿ-nʸeek, nʸee-cheh-VAW BYOO-shcheh-vuh-syah.

Only a tea cozy, nothing fragile.

526. Четыре рубля восемьдесят копеек. Вот ваша квитанция.

cheh-TIH-ryeh roob-LYAH VAW-syemʸ-dyeh-set kah-PЎEH-yek. vawt VAH-shah kvee-TAHN-tsee-yah.

4 rubles and 80 kopeks. Here is your receipt.

527. Спасибо.

spah-SʸEE-buh.

Thank you.

CHURCH

528. Is there an English-speaking priest here?
Есть ли здесь священник, говорящий по-
английски?
*yest^y l^yee zdyes^y svyah-SHCHEN-n^yeek guh-vah-
RYAH-shchee_ў puh-ahn-GL^yEE_Ῑ-sk^yee?*

529. —— a minister.
пастор.
PAH-stur.

530. —— a rabbi.
раввин.
rahv-V^yEEN.

531. A Catholic church.
Католическая церковь.
kah-tah-L^yEE-ches-kah-yah TSEHR-kuf^y.

532. A Protestant church.
Протестантская церковь.
pruh-tyeh-STAHNT-skah-yah TSEHR-kuf^y.

533. A Russian Orthodox church.
Русская православная церковь.
*ROOS-kah-yah prah-vah-SLAHV-nah-yah TSEHR-
kawf^y.*

534. A synagogue.
Синагога.
s^yee-nah-GAW-gah.

535. When is [the service] in the church?
Когда [служба в церкви]?
kahg-DAH [SLOOZH-bah f TSEHRK-v^yee]?

536. —— the mass.
обедня.
ah-BYED-nyah.

SIDE FIVE—BAND I
SIGHTSEEING

537. **We want a licensed guide who speaks English.**

Нам нужен официальный гид, говорящий по-английски.

nahm NOO-zhen uh-f ͭee-tsee-AHL ͭ-nih ͜ ў g ͭeed, guh-vah-RYAH-shchee ͜ ў puh-ahn-GL ͭEE ͜ Ŷ-sk ͭee.

538. **What is the charge [per hour]?**

Сколько это стоит [в час]?

SKAWL ͭ-kuh EH-tuh STAW- ͭeet [f chahs]?

539. —— **per day.**

в день.

v dyen ͭ.

540. **I am interested [in architecture].**

Меня интересует [архитектура].

myeh-NYAH een-tyeh-ryeh-SOO-yet [ahr-kh ͭee-tyek-TOO-rah].

541. —— **in painting.**

живопись.

ZHEE-vuh-p ͭees ͭ.

542. —— **in sculpture.**

скульптура.

skool ͭp-TOO-rah.

543. **Show us [the most important sights].**

Покажите нам [самые выдающиеся достопримечательности].

puh-kah-ZHEE-tyeh nahm [SAH-mih-yeh vih-dah-YOO-shchee-yeh-syah duh-stuh-pr ͭee-myeh-CHAH-tyel ͭ-nuh-st ͭee].

544. —— **the cathedral.**

собор.

sah-BAWR.

545. —— the museum.
музей.
moo-ZYEY̌.

546. When does it [open]?
Когда здесь [открывается]?
kahg-DAH zdyes^y [ut-krih-VAH-yeh-tsah]?

547. —— close.
закрывается.
zah-krih-VAH-yeh-tsah.

548. Where is [the entrance]?
Где здесь [вход]?
gdyeh zdyes^y [fkhawt]?

549. —— the exit.
выход.
VIH-khut.

550. The view is wonderful, isn't it?
Замечательный вид, не так ли?
zah-myeh-CHAN-tyel^y-nih‿y̆ v^yeet, nyeh tahk l^yee?

551. If there is time, let's rest a while.
Если есть время, дайте нам отдохнуть немного.
YES-l^yee yest^y VRYEH-myah, DAH‿Y̆-tyeh nahm ut-dahkh-NOOT^y nyeh-MNAW-guh.

AMUSEMENTS

552. I should like to go [to a concert].
Я хотел *m.*(хотела *f.*) бы пойти [на концерт].
yah khah-TYEL m.(*khah-TYEH-lah* f.) *bih pah‿y̆-T^yEE [nah kahn-TSEHRT].*

553. —— to a matinee.
на дневное представление.
nah dnyev-NAW-yeh pryet-stahv-LYEH-n^yee-yeh.

554. —— to the movies.
в кино.
ƒ k^{y}ee-NAW.

555. —— to a variety show.
в театр-варьете.
ƒ tyeh-AHTR-vahr^y-YEH-teh.

556. —— to the circus.
в цирк.
ƒ tseerk.

557. —— to the opera.
в оперу.
v AW-pyeh-roo.

558. —— to the ballet.
на балет.
nah bah-LYET.

559. —— to the Bolshoi Theater.
в Большой Театр.
v bahl^y-SHOЙ tyeh-AHTR.

560. —— to the box office.
в кассу театра.
ƒ KAHS-soo tyeh-AH-trah.

561. What is playing tonight?
Что идёт сегодня?
shtaw ee-DYAWT syeh-VAW-dnyah?

562. When does it begin?
Когда начало?
kahg-DAH nah-CHAH-luh?

563. How much is the admission charge?
Какая входная плата?
kah-KAH-yah ƒ khahd-NAH-yah PLAH-tah?

564. Have you seats [in the orchestra] for tonight?
Есть ли места [в партере] на сегодня?
yest^y l^yee myeh-STAH [f pahr-T^yEH-ryeh] nah syeh-VAW-dnyah?

565. —— in the balcony.
на балконе.
nah bahl-KAW-nyeh.

566. —— in a box.
в ложе.
v LAW-zheh.

567. Can I see and hear well from there?
Оттуда хорошо видно и слышно?
aht-TOO-dah khuh-rah-SHAW V^yEED-nuh ee SLIHSH-nuh?

568. When does the intermission begin?
Когда начнётся антракт?
kahg-DAH nahch-N^yAW-tsah ahn-TRAHKT?

569. Where can we go to dance?
Куда мы можем пойти потанцовать?
koo-DAH mih MAW-zhem pah‿y̆-T^yEE puh-tahn-tsah-VAHT^y?

570. May I have this dance? (*lit.* **Permit me to invite you for this dance**)
Разрешите пригласить вас на этот танец?
rahz-ryeh-SHEE-tyeh pr^yee-glah-S^yEET^y vahs nah EH-tut TAH-nyets?

SPORTS

571. Let's go [to the beach].
Давайте поедем [на пляж].
dah-VAH‿Y̆-tyeh pah-YEH-dyem [nah plyahsh].

572. —— to a soccer game.
на футбольный матч.
nah foot-BAWL^y-nih‿y̆ mahtch.

573. —— **to the races.**
на скачки.
nah SKAHCH-k^y*ee.*

574. —— **to the swimming pool.**
в плавательный бассейн.
f PLAH-vah-tyel^y*-nih_ў bahs-SYEĬN.*

575. **Can we go [fishing]?**
Можно нам поехать [ловить рыбу]?
MAWZH-nuh nahm pah-YEH-khaht^y *[lah-V*^{y}*EET*^{y}
RIH-boo]?

576. —— **horseback riding.**
кататься верхом.
kah-TAH-tsah vyehr-KHAWM.

577. —— **skating.**
кататься на коньках.
kah-TAH-tsah nah kahn^y*-KAHKH.*

578. —— **skiing.**
кататься на лыжах.
kah-TAH-tsah nah LIH-zhahkh.

579. —— **swimming.**
плавать.
PLAH-vaht^y*.*

580. **A fine idea!** (*lit.* **beautiful**)
Прекрасная мысль!
pryeh-KRAHS-nah-yah mihsl^y*!*

SIDE FIVE—BAND 2
BANK AND MONEY

581. **Where can I change foreign money?**
Где я могу обменять иностранную валюту?
gdyeh yah mah-GOO ub-myeh-NYAHT^y *ee-nah-*
STRAHN-noo-yoo vah-LYOO-too?

582. Where is the bank?
Где банк?
gdyeh bahnk?

583. Will you accept [my personal check]?
Вы примете [мой личный чек]?
vih PR^{y}EE-myeh-tyeh [moў L^{y}EECH-nih⌣ў chek]?

584. —— a traveler's check.
путевой чек.
poo-tyeh-VOЙ chek.

585. What is the exchange rate on the dollar today?
Какой курс доллара сегодня?
kah-KOЙ koors DAWL-lah-rah syeh-VAW-dnyah?

586. Can you change fifty dollars into rubles?
Вы можете обменять мне пятьдесят долларов на рубли?
vih MAW-zheh-tyeh ub-myeh-NYAHT^y mnyeh pyet^y-dyeh-SYAHT DAWL-lah-ruf nah roob-L^{y}EE?

587. Please give me [some large bills].
Пожалуйста дайте мне [крупными деньгами].
pah-ZHAH-loo-stah DAH⌣Ў-tyeh mnyeh [KROOP-nih-m^{y}ee dyen^y-GAH-m^{y}ee].

588. —— some small bills.
мелкими деньгами.
MYEL-k^{y}ee-m^{y}ee dyen^y-GAH-m^{y}ee.

589. —— some change.
немного мелочи.
nyeh-MNAW-guh MYEH-luh-chee.

SHOPPING*

590. I want to go shopping.
Я хочу пойти за покупками.
yah khah-CHOO pah_y̆-TʸEE zah pah-KOOP-kah-mʸee.

591. What do you wish?
Что вы желаете?
shtaw vih zheh-LAH-yeh-tyeh?

592. I do not like this one.
Мне это не нравится.
mnyeh EH-tuh nyeh NRAH-vʸee-tsah.

593. How much does this cost?
Сколько это стоит?
SKAWLʸ-kuh EH-tuh STAW-ʸeet?

594. The price is ten rubles and eighty-seven kopeks.
Цена десять рублей восемьдесят семь копеек.
tseh-NAH DYEH-syetʸ roob-LYEY̆ VAW-syemʸ-dyeh-syet syemʸ kah-PYEH-yek.

595. Is this the cheapest price?
Это самое дешёвое?
EH-tuh SAH-muh-yeh dyeh-SHAW-vuh-yeh?

596. Show me some others at a lower price.
Покажите мне другие подешевле.
puh-kah-ZHEE-tyeh mnyeh droo-GʸEE-yeh puh-dyeh-SHEV-lyeh.

* A vocabulary list of useful articles (unrecorded) appears in *Miscellaneous Articles*, Appendix II on pages 140–14 3.

597. I want something [better].
Я хочу что-нибудь [получше].
yah khah-CHOO SHTAW-nee-boot^y *[pah-LOOCH-sheh].*

598. —— cheaper.
подешевле.
puh-dyeh-SHEV-lyeh.

599. —— larger.
побольше.
pah-BAWL^y*-sheh.*

600. —— smaller.
поменьше.
pah-MYEN^y*-sheh.*

601. —— stronger.
посильнее.
puh-s^y*eel*^{y}*-NYEH-yeh.*

602. May I try this on?
Можно мне это примерить?
MAWZH-nuh mnyeh EH-tuh pr^y*ee-MYEN-r*^{y}*eet*^{y}*?*

603. Can I order the same thing in another size?
Могу я заказать точно такое другого
размера?
mah-GOO yah zah-kah-ZAHT^y *TAWCH-nuh tah-KAW-yeh droo-GAW-vuh rahz-MYEH-rah?*

604. Please take the measurements.
Пожалуйста снимите мерку.
pah-ZHAH-loo-stah sn^y*ee-M*^{y}*EE-tyeh MYEHR-koo.*

605. The length and width.
Длина и ширина.
dl^y*ee-NAH ee shee-r*^{y}*ee-NAH.*

606. How much time do you need to make it?
Сколько времени нужно чтобы это сделать?
SKAWL^y*-kuh VRYEH-myeh-n*^{y}*ee NOOZH-nuh SHTAW-bih EH-tuh SDYEH-laht*^{y}*?*

607. I'll return a little later.
Я вернусь через некоторое время.
yah vyehr-NOOS^y CHEN-ryez NYEH-kuh-tuh-ruh-yeh VRYEH-myah.

608. Can you ship it to New York?
Можете ли вы отправить зто в Нью Йорк?
MAW-zheh-tyeh lee vih aht-PRAH-v^yeet^y EH-tuh f " New York "?

609. Do I pay [the salesgirl]?
Платить [продавщице]?
plah-T^yEET^y [pruh-dahf-SHCHEE-tseh]?

610. —— the salesman.
продавцу.
pruh-dahf-TSOO.

611. —— at the cashier's.
в кассу.
f KAHS-soo.

612. Please give me a bill for all the purchases.
Пожалуйста дайте мне чек на все покупки.
pah-ZHAN-loo-stah DAH＿Ỹ-tyeh mnyeh chek nah fsyeh pah-KOOP-k^yee.

613. Please wrap it carefully for export.
Пожалуйста упакуйте хорошенько для отправки.
pah-ZHAN-loo-stah oo-pah-KOO＿Ỹ-tyeh khuh-rah-SHEN^y-kuh dlyah aht-PRAHF-k^yee.

SIDE FIVE—BAND 3
CLOTHING

614. I want to buy [a bathing cap].
Я хочу купить [купальный чепчик].
yah khah-CHOO koo-P^yEET^y [koo-PHAL^y-nih＿ў CHEP-cheek].

615. —— **a bathing suit.**
купальный костюм.
koo-PAHL^y-nih‿ў kahs-TYOOM.

616. —— **a cotton blouse.**
ситцевую блузку.
S^{y}EET-tseh-voo-yoo BLOOS-koo.

617. —— **a brassière.**
лифчик.
L^{y}EEF-cheek.

618. —— **an overcoat.**
пальто.
pahl^y-TAW.

619. —— **a dress.**
платье.
PLAHT^y-yeh.

620. —— **some children's dresses.**
детские платья.
DYET-sk^{y}ee-yeh PLAHT^y-yah.

621. —— **a pair of galoshes.**
пару галош.
PAH-roo gah-LAWSH.

622. —— **a pair of garters.**
пару подвязок.
PAH-roo pahd-VYAH-zuk.

623. —— **a girdle.**
пояс с резинками.
PAW-yahs s ryeh-Z^{y}EEN-kah-m^{y}ee.

624. —— **a pair of gloves.**
пару перчаток.
PAH-roo pyehr-CHAH-tuk.

625. —— **a handbag.**
сумочку.
SOO-much-koo.

626. —— **one dozen handkerchiefs.**
дюжину носовых платков.
DYOO-zhee-noo nuh-sah-VIHKH plaht-KAWF.

627. —— **a hat.**
шляпу.
SHLYAH-poo.

628. —— **a jacket.**
жакет.
zhah-KYET.

629. —— **some lingerie.**
дамское бельё.
DAHM-skuh-yeh byel^y-YAW.

630. —— **underwear (men's).**
мужское бельё.
moosh-SKAW-yeh byel^y-YAW.

631. —— **a nightgown.**
ночную рубашку.
nahch-NOO-yoo roo-BAHSH-koo.

632. —— **a raincoat.**
дождевой плащ.
duzh-dyeh-VOЎ plahshch.

633. —— **a pair of ladies' shoes.**
пару туфель.
PAH-roo TOO-fyel^y.

634. —— **a pair of men's shoes.**
пару ботинок.
PAH-roo bah-T^yEE-nuk.

635. —— **some shoelaces.**
шнурки для ботинок.
shnoor-K^yEE dlyah bah-T^yEE-nuk.

636. —— **a skirt.**
юбку.
YOOP-koo.

637. —— **a pair of house slippers.**
пару домашних туфель.
PAH-roo dah-MAHSH-nʸeekh TOO-fyelʸ.

638. —— **a shirt.**
рубашку.
roo-BAHSH-koo.

639. —— **a pair of socks.**
пару носков.
PAH-roo nahs-KAWF.

640. —— **a pair of nylon stockings.**
пару капроновых чулок.
PAH-roo kah-PRAW-nuh-vihkh choo-LAWK.

641. —— **a suit.**
костюм.
kahs-TYOOM.

642. —— **a woolen sweater.**
шерстяной светер.
shehr-styah-NOĬ SVYEH-tehr.

643. —— **some neckties.**
галстуки.
GAHL-stoo-kʸee.

644. —— **a pair of trousers.**
пару брюк.
PAH-roo bryook.

645. —— **a coat (suit).**
пиджак.
pʸee-DZHAHK.

COLORS

646. Show me [a lighter shade].
Покажите мне [более светлый оттенок].
*puh-kah-ZHʸEE-tyeh mnyeh [BAW-lyeh-yeh SVYET-
lih‿ў aht-TYEH-nuk].*

647. —— a darker shade (color).
более тёмный оттенок (цвет).
BAW-lyeh-yeh   TYAWM-nih‿ў   aht-TYEH-nuk (tsvyet).

648. Black.
Чёрный.
CHAWR-nih‿ў.

649. Blue.
Голубой.
guh-loo-BOЎ.

650. Dark blue.
Синий.
SʸEE-nʸee‿ў.

651. Brown.
Коричневый.
kah-RʸEECH-nyeh-vih‿ў.

652. Gray.
Серый.
SYEH-rih‿ў.

653. Green.
Зелёный.
zyeh-LYAW-nih‿ў.

654. Orange.
Оранжевый.
ah-RAHN-zheh-vih‿ў.

655. Pink.
Розовый.
RAW-zuh-vih‿ў.

656. Purple.
Фиолетовый.
fʸee-ah-LYEH-tuh-vih‿ў.

657. Red.
Красный.
KRAHS-nih‿ў.

658. White.
Белый.
BYEH-lih⌣ў.

659. Yellow.
Жёлтый.
ZHAWL-tih⌣ў.

STORES*

660. Where can I find [a bakery]?
Где я смогу найти [хлебную лавку]?
gdyeh yah smah-GOO nah⌣ў-TᵞEE [KHLYEB-noo-yoo LAHF-koo]?

661. —— a candy and pastry store.
кондитерскую.
kahn-DᵞEE-tyehr-skoo-yoo.

662. —— a cigar store.
табачную лавку.
tah-BAHCH-noo-yoo LAHF-koo.

663. —— a ready-to-wear clothing store.
магазин готового платья.
mah-gah-ZᵞEEN gah-TAW-vuh-vuh PLAHTᵞ-yah.

664. —— a department store.
универмаг.
oo-nᵞee-vyehr-MAHK.

665. —— a pharmacy.
аптеку.
ahp-TYEH-koo.

* An extensive list (unrecorded) of additional stores and public services appears in *Signs and Public Notices*, Appendix VII, on pages 159–177.

666. —— **a grocery store.**
бакалейную лавку.
bah-kah-LYEЎ-noo-yoo LAHF-koo.

667. —— **a hardware store.**
скобяную лавку.
skuh-byah-NOO-yoo LAHF-koo.

668. —— **a hat shop.**
магазин шляп.
mah-gah-ZᵞEEN shlyahp.

669. —— **a jewelry store.**
ювелирный магазин.
yoo-vyeh-LᵞEER-nih_ў mah-gah-ZᵞEEN.

670. —— **a dry goods store.**
галантерейный магазин.
gah-lyahn-tyeh-RYEЎ-nih_ў mah-gah-ZᵞEEN.

671. —— **a market place.**
рынок.
RIH-nuk.

672. —— **a meat market.**
мясной рынок.
myahs-NOЎ RIH-nuk.

673. —— **a shoemaker.**
сапожника.
sah-PAWZH-nᵞee-kah.

674. —— **a shoe store.**
обувной магазин.
uh-boov-NOЎ mah-gah-ZᵞEEN.

675. —— **a custom made clothing store.**
пошивочную мастерскую.
pah-SHᵞEE-vuch-noo-yoo mahs-tyehr-SKOO-yoo.

676. —— **a watch maker.**
часовщика.
chah-suf-shchee-KAH.

677. —— a tailor.
портного.
pahrt-NAW-vuh.

SIDE SIX—BAND I
BOOKSTORE AND STATIONER'S

678. Where is there [a bookstore]?
Где здесь [книжный магазин]?
gdyeh zdyes^y [KN^yEEZH-nih_ў mah-gah-Z^yEEN]?

679. —— a stationer's.
писчебумажный магазин.
p^yee-shcheh-boo-MAHZH-nih_ў mah-gah-Z^yEEN.

680. —— a newsstand.
газетный киоск.
gah-ZYET-nih_ў k^yee-AWSK.

681. I want to buy [a book].
Я хочу купить [книгу].
yah khah-CHOO koo-P^yEET^y [KN^yEE-goo].

682. —— a guidebook.
путеводитель.
poo-tyeh-vah-D^yEE-tyel^y.

683. —— a dictionary.
словарь.
slah-VAHR^y.

684. —— a magazine.
журнал.
zhoor-NAHL.

685. —— a newspaper.
газету.
gah-ZYEH-too.

686. —— **a map of the Soviet Union.**
карту Советского Союза.
KAHR-too sah-VYET-skuh-vuh sah-YOO-zah.

687. I need some [envelopes].
Мне нужны [конверты].
mnyeh noozh-NIH [kahn-VYEHR-tih].

688. —— **postcards.**
почтовые открытки.
pahch-TAW-vih-yeh aht-KRIHT-kʸee.

689. —— **ink.**
чернила.
chehr-Nʸ EE-lah.

690. I need a pencil.
Мне нужен карандаш.
mnyeh NOO-zhen kah-rahn-DAHSH.

691. —— **string.**
шпагат.
shpah-GAHT.

692. I need a fountain pen.
Мне нужно вечное перо.
mnyeh NOOZH-nuh VYECH-nuh-yeh pyeh-RAW.

693. I need some writing paper.
Мне нужна почтовая бумага.
mnyeh noozh-NAH pahch-TAW-vah-yah boo-MAH-gah.

694. —— **wrapping paper.**
обёрточная бумага.
ah-BYAWR-tuch-nah-yah boo-MAH-gah.

CIGAR STORE

695. Where is the nearest cigar store?
Где здесь ближайшая табачная лавка?
gdyeh zdyesʸ blʸee-ZHAH Ῐ-shah-yah tah-BAHCH-nah-yah LAHF-kah?

696. What kind of cigars do you have?
Какие у вас есть сигары?
kah-KʸEE-yeh oo vahs yestʸ sʸee-GAH-rih?

**697. I want to buy [a pack of American
cigarettes].**
Я хочу купить [пачку американских
папирос].
*yah khah-CHOO koo-PʸEETʸ [PAHCH-koo ah-
myeh-rʸee-KAHN-skʸeekh pah-pʸee-RAWS].*

698. —— a leather cigarette case.
кожаный портсигар.
KAW-zhah-nih_y̆ purt-sʸee-GAHR.

699. —— a lighter.
зажигалку.
zah-zhee-GAHL-koo.

700. —— some pipe tobacco.
табаку для трубки.
tah-bah-KOO dlyah TROOP-kʸee.

701. Do you have a match? (*lit.* **Will you find a
match?**)
У вас найдётся спичка?
oo vahs nah_y̆-DYAW-tsah SPʸEECH-kah?

CAMERA STORE

702. I want a roll of film for this camera.
Мне нужна катушка плёнки вот для этого
фото-аппарата.
*mnyeh noozh-NAH kah-TOOSH-kah PLYAWN-kʸee
vawt dlyah EH-tuh-vuh FAW-tuh-ah-pah-RAH-tah.*

703. **How much do you charge for developing color films?**

Сколько вы берёте за проявление цветной плёнки?

SKAWL-kuh vih byeh-RYAW-tyeh zah pruh-yahv-LYEH-n^yee-yeh tsvyet-NOY̆ PLYAWN-k^yee?

704. When will they be ready?

Когда будет готово?

kahg-DAH BOO-dyet gah-TAW-vuh?

705. May I take a snapshot of you?

Можно мне вас сфотографировать?

MAWZH-nuh mnyeh vahs sfuh-tuh-grah-F^yEE-ruh-vaht^y?

PHARMACY*

706. Do you know a pharmacy where they speak English?

Знаете вы аптеку, где говорят по-английски?

ZNAH-yeh-tyeh vih ahp-TYEH-koo, gdyeh guh-vah-RYAHT puh-ahn-GL^yEE_Y̆-sk^yee?

707. Do you have some aspirin?

У вас есть аспирин?

oo vahs yest^y ahs-p^yee-R^yEEN?

708. I want to speak to [a male clerk].

Я хочу поговорить с [продавцом].

yah khah-CHOO puh-guh-vah-R^yEET^y s [pruh-dahf-TSAWM].

709. —— a female clerk.

продавщицей.

pruh-dahf-SHCHEE-tsey̆.

---

* An extensive list (unrecorded) of *Drugs, Cosmetics and Personal Accessories* appears in Appendix III, on pages 143–147.

710. Can you fill this prescription immediately?
Вы сможете приготовить мне этот рецепт немедленно?
vih SMAW-zheh-tyeh prʸee-gah-TAW-vʸeetʸ mnyeh EH-tut ryeh-TSEPT nyeh-MYED-lyen-nuh?

711. I shall wait.
Я подожду.
yah puh-dah-ZHDOO.

SIDE SIX—BAND 2
LAUNDRY AND DRY CLEANING

712. Where is [the laundry] here?
Где здесь [прачечная]?
gdyeh zdyesʸ [PRAH-chesh-nah-yah]?

713. —— the dry cleaning service.
химическая чистка.
khʸee-MʸEE-cheh-skah-yah CHEEST-kah.

714. These shirts must be washed and mended.
Эти рубашки нужно выстирать и заштопать.
EH-tee roo-BAHSH-kʸee NOOZH-nuh VIH-stʸee-rahtʸ ee zah-SHTAW-pahtʸ.

715. Do not starch.
Не крахмальте.
nyeh krahkh-MAHLʸ-tyeh.

716. This suit must be cleaned and pressed.
Этот костюм нужно вычистить и выгладить.
EH-tut kahs-TYOOM NOOZH-nuh VIH-chees-tʸeetʸ ee VIH-glah-dʸeetʸ.

717. The belt is missing.
Не хватает пояса.
nyeh khvah-TAH-yet PAW-yah-sah.

718. Can you [sew on this button]?
Можете вы [пришить мне эту пуговицу]?
MAW-zheh-tyeh vih [pr.^yee-SHEET^y mnyeh EH-too POO-guh-v^yee-tsoo].?

719. —— put in a new zipper.
вставить новую застёжку молнию.
FSTAH-veet^y ÑAW-voo-yoo zah-STYAWSH-KOO MAWL-n^yee-yoo.

BARBER SHOP AND BEAUTY SALON

720. Where is there [a hairdresser]?
Где здесь [дамская парикмахерская]?
gdyeh zdyes^y [DAHM-skah-yah pah-r^yeek-MAH-khyehr-skah-yah].?

721. —— a barber shop.
мужская парикмахерская.
moosh-SKAH-yah pah-r^yeek-MAH-khyehr-skah-yah.

722. —— a beauty salon.
косметический кабинет.
kus-myeh-T^yEE-cheh-sk^yee_y̆ KAH-b^yee-nyet.

723. A haircut, please.
Постричь, пожалуйста.
pah-STR^yEECH, pah-ZHAH-loo-stah.

724. Not too short.
Не слишком коротко.
nyeh SL^yEESH-kum KAW-rut-kuh.

725. No lotion.
Не надо помады.
nyeh ÑAH-duh pah-MAH-dih.

726. Give me a shave, please.
Побрейте меня, пожалуйста.
pah-BRYEY̆-tyeh myeh-ÑYAH, pah-ZHAH-loo-stah.

727. Wash my hair. (*lit.* **head**)
Вымойте мне голову.
VIH-moў-tyeh mnyeh GAW-luh-voo.

728. Set my hair.
Уложите мне волосы.
oo-luh-ZHEE-tyeh mnyeh VAW-luh-sih.

729. Give me a [permanent] please.
Сделайте мне [перманент] пожалуйста.
ZDYEH-lah‿ў-tyeh mnyeh [pyehr-mah-NYENT] pah-ZHAH-loo-stah.

730. —— a facial.
массаж лица.
mahs-SAHZH lʸee-TSAH.

731. —— a head massage.
массаж головы.
mahs-SAHZH guh-lah-VIH.

732. —— a manicure.
маникюр.
mah-nʸee-KYOOR.

HEALTH AND ILLNESS

733. I want to go to see an American doctor.
Я хочу пойти к американскому доктору.
yah khah-CHOO pah‿ў-TʸEE k ah-myeh-rʸee-KAHN-skuh-moo DAWK-tuh-roo.

734. Is the doctor in? (*lit.* **Does the doctor receive?**)
Доктор принимает?
DAWK-tur prʸee-nʸee-MAH-yet?

735. I have [a headache].
У меня болит [голова].
oo myeh-NYAH bah-LYEET [guh-lah-VAH].

736. —— **a sore throat.** (*lit.* **throat**)
горло.
GAWR-luh.

737. I have [**a cold**].
У меня [простуда].
oo myeh-NYAH [*prah-STOO-dah*].

738. —— **a cough.**
кашель.
KAH-shel^y.

739. —— **a fever.**
лихорадка.
l^yee-khah-RAHT-kah.

740. —— **nausea.**
тошнота.
tush-nah-TAH.

741. —— **constipation.**
запор.
zah-PAWR.

742. —— **diarrhoea.**
понос.
pah-NAWS.

743. —— **indigestion.**
расстройство желудка.
rahs-STROY̆-stvuh zheh-LOOT-kah.

744. —— **pain in my chest.**
боль в груди.
BAWL^y v groo-D^yEE.

745. There is something in my eye. (*lit.* **Something got into my eye.**)
Мне что-то попало в глаз.
mnyeh SHTAW-tuh pah-PAH-luh v glahs.

746. I sleep poorly.
Я плохо сплю.
yah PLAW-khuh splyoo.

747. How do you feel?
Как вы себя чувствуете?
kahk vih syeh-BYAH CHOO-stvoo-yeh-tyeh?

748. I feel [well].
Я чувствую себя [хорошо].
yah CHOO-stvoo-yoo syeh-BYAH [khuh-rah-SHAW].

749. —— better.
лучше.
LOOCH-sheh.

750. —— worse.
хуже.
KHOO-zheh.

751. Must I stay in bed?
Мне нужно лежать в кровати?
mnyeh NOOZH-nuh lyeh-ZHAHT^y f krah-VAH-t^yee?

752. When shall I be able to continue my trip?
Когда я смогу продолжать поездку?
kahg-DAH yah smah-GOO pruh-dahl-ZHAHT^y puh-YEZT-koo?

DENTIST

753. Do you know a good dentist?
Вы знаете хорошего зубного врача?
vih ZNAH-yeh-tyeh khah-RAW-sheh-vuh zoob-NAW-vuh vrah-CHAH?

754. This tooth hurts.
У меня болит этот зуб.
oo myeh-NYAH bah-L^yEET EH-tut zoop.

755. I seem to have lost the filling.

Я, кажется, потерял *m.* (потеряла *f.*) пломбу.

yah, KAH-zheh-tsah, puh-tyeh-RYAL m. *(puh-tyeh-RYAH-lah* f.) *PLAWM-boo.*

756. Can you fix it temporarily?

Сможете ли вы подлечить его на время?

SMAW-zheh-tyeh lʸee vih pud-lyeh-CHEETʸ yeh-VAW nah VRYEH-myah?

757. I do not want you to pull it out.

Я не хочу, что бы вы его вырвали.

yah nyeh khah-CHOO shtaw bih vih yeh-VAW VIHR-vah-lʸee.

SIDE SIX—BAND 3
TIME

758. What time is it?

Который час?

kah-TAW-rih_ў chahs?

759. It is very early.

Очень рано.

AW-chenʸ RAH-nuh.

760. It is too late.

Слишком поздно.

SLʸEESH-kum PAWZ-nuh.

761. It is almost two o'clock A.M. (P.M.)*

Почти два часа. (Четырнадцать часов).

pah-CHTʸEE dvah chah-SAH. (cheh-TIHR-nah-tsahtʸ chah-SAWF).

762. It is half past three. (*lit.* **half to four**)

Половина четвёртого.

puh-lah-VʸEE-nah chet-VYAWR-tuh-vuh.

---

* The twenty-four hour system is more commonly used in Europe than in the United States.   One to twelve P.M. are therefore expressed in numbers from thirteen to twenty-four.

763. It is a quarter past four. (*lit.* **a quarter towards five**)
Четверть пятого.
*CHET-vyehrt*ʸ *PYAH-tuh-vuh.*

764. It is a quarter to five.
Без четверти пять.
*byez CHET-vyehr-t*ʸ*ee pyaht*ʸ*.*

765. Ten to six.
Без десяти шесть.
*byez dyeh-syeh-T*ʸ*EE shest*ʸ*.*

766. At twenty minutes past seven. (*lit.* **twenty towards eight**)
В двадцать минут восмого.
*v DVAH-tset*ʸ *m*ʸ*ee-NOOT vahs*ʸ*-MAW-vuh.*

767. In the morning.
Утром.
OOT-rum.

768. In the afternoon.
Днём.
dnyawm.

769. In the evening.
Вечером.
VYEH-cheh-rum.

770. Last year. В прошлом году.
f PRAWSH-lum gah-DOO.

771. Last month. В прошлом месяце.
f PRAWSH-lum MYEH-syah-tseh.

772. Last night. Вчера вечером.
fcheh-RAH VYEH-cheh-rum.

773. Night. Ночь. *nawch.*

774. Tonight. Сегодня вечером.
syeh-VAW-dnyah VYEH-cheh-rum.

775. Yesterday. Вчера. *fcheh-RAH.*

776. Today. Сегодня. *syeh-VAW-dnyah.*

777. Day. День. *dyen^y.*

778. Tomorrow. Завтра. *ZAHF-trah.*

779. Next week. На следующей неделе.
nah SLYEH-doo-yoo-shchey nyeh-DYEH-lyeh.

DAYS OF THE WEEK

780. Monday. Понедельник. *puh-nyeh-DYEL^y-n^yeek.*

781. Tuesday. Вторник. *FTAWR-n^yeek.*

782. Wednesday. Среда. *sryeh-DAH.*

783. Thursday. Четверг. *chet-VYEHRK.*

784. Friday. Пятница. *PYAHT-n^yee-tsah.*

785. Saturday. Суббота. *soo-BAW-tah.*

786. Sunday. Воскресенье. *vuh-skryeh-SYEN^y-yeh.*

MONTHS

787. January. Январь. *yahn-VAHR^y.*

788. February. Февраль. *fyev-RAHL^y.*

789. March. Март. *mahrt.*

790. April. Апрель. *ahp-RYEL^y.*

791. May. Май. *mah‿y̆.*

792. June. Июнь. *ee-YOON^y.*

793. July. Июль. *ee-YOOL^y.*

794. August. Август. *AHV-goost.*

795. September. Сентябрь. *syen-TYAHBR^y.*

796. October. Октябрь. *ahk-TYAHBR^y.*

797. November. Ноябрь. *nah-YAHBR^y.*

798. December. Декабрь. *dyeh-KAHBR^y.*

SEASONS AND WEATHER

799. Spring. Весна. *vyes-NAH.*

800. Summer. Лето. *LYEH-tuh.*

801. Autumn. Осень. *AW-syen^y.*

802. Winter. Зима. *z^yee-MAH.*

803. It is warm. Тепло. *tyep-LAW.*

804. It is cold. Холодно. *KHAW-lud-nuh.*

805. It is raining.
Идёт дождь.
ee-DYAWT dawsht^y.

806. It is snowing.
Идёт снег.
ee-DYAWT snyek.

807. The weather is good.
Погода хорошая.
pah-GAW-duh khah-RAW-shah-yah.

808. The weather is bad.
Погода плохая.
pah-GAW-duh plah-KHAH-yah.

809. The weather is sunny.
Погода солнечная.
pah-GAW-duh SAWL-nyech-nah-yah.

810. The weather is windy.
Погода ветреная.
pah-GAW-dah VYET-ryeh-nah-yah.

811. What is the weather forecast for tomorrow?
Каково предсказание погоды на завтра?
kah-kah-VAW pryet-skah-ZAH-n^yee-yeh pah-GAW-dih nah ZAHF-trah?

NUMBERS*

812. One. Один (одна, одно).
ah-D^yEEN (ah-DNAH, ah-DNAW).

Two. Два (две). *dvah (dvyeh).*

Three. Три. *tr^yee.*

Four. Четыре. *cheh-TIH-ryeh.*

Five. Пять. *pyaht^y.*

Six. Шесть. *shest^y.*

Seven. Семь. *syem^y.*

Eight. Восемь. *VAW-syem^y.*

Nine. Девять. *DYEH-vyet^y.*

Ten. Десять. *DYEH-syet^y.*

Eleven. Одиннадцать. *ah-D^yEE-nah-tsaht^y.*

Twelve. Двенадцать. *dvyeh-NAH-tsaht^y.*

Thirteen. Тринадцать. *tr^yee-NAH-tsaht^y.*

Fourteen. Четырнадцать.
cheh-TIHR-nah-tsaht^y.

Fifteen. Пятнадцать. *pyeht-NAH-tsaht^y.*

Sixteen. Шестнадцать. *shest-NAH-tsaht^y.*

Seventeen. Семнадцать. *syem-NAH-tsaht^y.*

* All Russian numbers are declined. The forms given here (in the nominative case) are used for counting.

Eighteen. Восемнадцать.
vuh-syem-NAH-tsaht^y.

Nineteen. Девятнадцать.
dyeh-vyet-NAH-tsaht^y.

Twenty. Двадцать. *DVAH-tsaht^y*.

Twenty-one. Двадцать один (одна, одно).
DVAH-tsaht^y ah-D^yEEN (ah-DNAH, ah-DNAW).

Twenty-two. Двадцать два (две).
DVAH-tsaht^y dvah (dvyeh).

Thirty. Тридцать. *TR^yEE-tsaht^y*.

Forty. Сорок. *SAW-ruk*.

Fifty. Пятьдесят. *pet^y-dyeh-SYAHT*.

Sixty. Шестьдесят. *shest^y-dyeh-SYAHT*.

Seventy. Семьдесят. *SYEM^y-dyeh-syet*.

Eighty. Восемьдесят. *VAW-syem^y-dyeh-syet*.

Ninety. Девяносто. *dyeh-vyeh-NAW-stuh*.

One hundred. Сто. *staw*.

Two hundred. Двести. *DVYEH-st^yee*.

Three hundred. Триста. *TR^yEE-stah*.

Four hundred. Четыреста.
cheh-TIH-ryeh-stah.

Five hundred. Пятьсот. *pet^y-SAWT*.

Six hundred. Шестьсот. *shest^y-SAWT*.

Seven hundred. Семьсот. *syem^y-SAWT*.

Eight hundred. Восемьсот. *vuh-syem^y-SAWT*.

Nine hundred. Девятьсот. *dyeh-vyet^y-SAWT*.

One thousand.   Одна тысяча.
ah-DNAH TIH-syeh-chah.

Two thousand.   Две тысячи.
dvyeh TIH-syeh-chee.

Five thousand.   Пять тысяч.
pyaht^y TIH-syahch.

One million.   Один миллион.
ah-D^{y}EEN m^{y}eel^y-YAWN.

Two million.   Два миллиона.
dvah m^{y}eel^y-l^{y}ee-AW-nah.

Six million.   Шесть миллионов.
shest^y m^{y}eel^y-l^{y}ee-AW-nuf.

APPENDIX I (not recorded)
NATIVE FOOD AND DRINK LIST
ALCOHOLIC DRINKS*

813. Red table wines.
Вина столовые красные.
V^{y}EE-nah stah-LAW-vih-yeh KRAHS-nih-yeh.

Абрау-Каберне.
*ahb-RAH-oo kah-BYEHR-NEH.**

Грузинское № 4.
groo-Z^{y}EEN-skuh-yeh NAW-myehr cheh-TIH-ryeh.

Грузинское № 5.
groo-Z^{y}EEN-skuh-yeh NAW-myehr pyaht^y.

Кахетинское красное.
kah-khyeh-T^{y}EEN-skuh-yeh KRAHS-nuh-yeh.

* English translation is not given where there is no familiar
English counterpart.

Матрасса.
mah-TRAH-sah.

Шамхор.
shahm-KHAWR.

814. White table wines.
Вина столовые белые.
V^yEE-nah stah-LAW-vih-yeh BYEH-lih-yeh.

Абрау-Рислинг.
ahb-RAH-oo-R^yEES-l^yeeng. Riesling.

Анапа-Рислинг.
ah-NAH-pah-R^yEES-l^yeeng. Riesling.

Грузинское № 1.
groo-Z^yEEN-skuh-yeh NAW-myehr ah-D^yEEN.

Грузинское № 3.
groo-Z^yEEN-skuh-yeh NAW-myehr tr^yee.

Грузинское № 12.
groo-Z^yEEN-skuh-yeh NAW-myehr dveh-NAH-tsaht^y.

Кахетинское белое.
kah-khyeh-T^yEEN-skuh-yeh BYEH-luh-yeh.

Садилы.
sah-d^yee-LIH.

Сотерн.
sah-TYEHRN. Sauternes.

Ясман-Салык.
yahs-MAHN-sah-LIHK.

Шампанское.
shahm-PAHN-skuh-yeh. Champagne.

815. Port wines.
Портвейны.
pahrt-VYEY̌-nih.

Ливадия. *l^yee-VAH-d^yee-yah.*

Массандра.   *mahs-SAHN-drah.*

Южнобережный белый.
yoozh-nuh-byeh-RYEZH-nih⏑ў BYEH-lih⏑ў.

816. Dessert wines.
Вина десертные.
V^yEE-nah dyeh-SYEHRT-nih-yeh.

Айгешат.   *ah⏑ў-gyeh-SHAHT.*

Акстафа.   *ahk-stah-FAH.*

Алеатико.   *ah-lyeh-AH-t^yee-kuh.*

Барзак.   *bahr-ZAHK.*   Barsac.

Кагор.   *kah-GAWR.*

Мадера.   *mah-DYEH-rah.*   Madeira.

Мускат.   *moos-KAHT.*

Мускатель.   *moos-kah-TYEL^y.*   Muscatel.

Тер-Баш.   *tyehr-bahsh.*

Токай.   *tah-KAH⏑Ў.*   Tokay.

Херес.   *KHYEH-ryes.*   Sherry.

Шато-Икем.   *shah-TAW-^yee-KYEM.*   Château Yquem.

817. Fruit liqueur.
Наливка.
nah-LEEF-kah.

Вишнёвая.   *v^yeesh-NYAW-vah-yah.*   Cherry.

Малиновая.   *mah-L^yEE-nuh-vuh-yah.*
Raspberry.

Сливянка.   *sl^yee-VYAHN-kah.*   Plum.

Запеканка.   *zah-pyeh-KAHN-kah.*
Spiced brandy.

818. Herb liqueur.
Настойка.
nah-STOЎ-kah.

зубровка.　*zoob-RAWF-kah.*　Sweet grass.

спотыкач.　*spuh-tih-KAHCH.*　Mixed herbs.

819. Vodka.
Водка.
VAWT-kah.

HORS D'ŒUVRES AND SNACKS*

820. Анчоусы.
ahn-CHAW-oo-sih.
Anchovies.

821. Балык.
bah-LIHK.
Cured back of sturgeon.

822. Буженина.
boo-zheh-NᵞEE-nah.
Cold pork, boiled first then roasted.

823. Бутерброд (с колбасой, с сыром, с икрой
с ветчиной).
*boo-tᵞehr-BRAWT(s kuhl-bah-SOY̆, s SIH-rum, s
eek-ROY̆) s vyet-chee-NOY̆.*
Open sandwich (with sausage, with cheese, with
caviar, with ham).

824. Закуски.
zah-KOO-skᵞee.
Hors d'œuvres.

825. Икра.
eek-RAH.
Roe caviar.

826. Кетовая икра.
KYEH-tuh-vah-yah eek-RAH.
Salmon roe caviar (red caviar).

* All foods are alphabetized according to the Russian alphabet
to facilitate the reading of Russian menus.

827. Чёрная икра.
CHAWR-nah-yah eek-RAH.
Sturgeon roe caviar.

828. Зернистая икра.
zyehr-N^{y}EE-stah-yah eek-RAH.
Fresh caviar.

829. Паюсная икра.
PAH-yoos-nah-yah eek-RAH.
Pressed caviar.

830. Кета.
KYEH-tah.
Salmon.

831. Кильки.
K^{y}EEL^y-k^{y}ee.
Sprats in brine.

832. Колбаса (ливерная).
kuhl-bah-SAH (L^{y}EE-vyehr-nah-yah).
Sausage (liver).

833. Копчёная селёдка.
kahp-CHAW-nah-yah syeh-LYAWT-kah.
Smoked herring.

834. Лососина.
luh-sah-S^{y}EE-nah.
Lox (smoked salmon).

835. Маринованная селёдка.
mah-r^{y}ee-NAW-vahn-nah-yah syeh-LYAWT-kah.
Pickled herring.

836. Майонез из дичи.
may‿ў-ah-NEZ eez D^{y}EE-chee.
Game in mayonnaise.

837. Миноги.
m^{y}ee-NAW-g^{y}ee.
Smoked lampreys.

838. Московская.
mahs-KAWF-skah-yah.
Hard salami.

839. Окорок.
AW-kuh-ruk.
Ham (usually the whole hind leg).

840. Осетрина заливная.
uh-syet-RʸEE-nah zah-lʸeev-NAH-yah.
Jellied sturgeon.

841. Помидоры фаршированные салатом.
puh-mʸee-DAW-rih fahr-shee-RAW-vahn-nih-yeh sah-LAH-tum.
Tomatoes stuffed with mixed salad.

842. Поросёнок заливной.
puh-rah-SYAW-nuk zah-lʸeev-NOY̆.
Jellied suckling pig.

843. Рубленная печёнка.
ROOB-lyen-nah-yah pyeh-CHAWN-kah.
Chopped liver.

844. Сардельки.
sahr-DYELʸ-kʸee.
Large wieners.

845. Сандвич.
SAHND-vʸeech.
Sandwich.

846. Селёдка с гарниром.
syeh-LYAWT-kah s gahr-NʸEE-rum.
Garnished salt herring.

847. Сёмга.
SYAWM-gah.
Smoked salmon.

848. Сосиски.
sah-S^{y}EES-k^{y}ee.
Wieners.

849. Чайная.
CHAH_Ў-nah-yah.
Bologna.

850. Шпроты.
SHPRAW-tih.
Smoked sprats in oil.

851. Язык копчёный.
yah-ZIHK kahp-CHAW-nih_ў.
Smoked tongue.

BREADS AND PASTRY

852. Батон.
bah-TAWN.
French bread.

853. Бублики.
BOOB-l^{y}ee-k^{y}ee.
Rings of dough scalded and baked.

854. Булочки.
BOO-luch-k^{y}ee.
Rolls.

855. Булочки сдобные.
BOO-luch-k^{y}ee ZDAWB-nih-yeh.
Sweet (tea) rolls.

856. Варенники с мясом, с кислой капустой, с
вишнями, с творогом.
*vah-RYEN-n^{y}ee-k^{y}ee, s MYAH-sum, s K^{y}EES-loў
kah-POOS-toў, s V^{y}EESH-nyah-m^{y}ee, s tvuh-rah-
GAWM.*
Dumplings filled with meat, sauerkraut; cherries,
or cottage cheese (served with melted butter
and sour cream). .

857. Ватрушки (с рыбой, с творогом, с вареньем).
vah-TROOSH-k^{y}ee (s RIH-boў, s tvuh-rah-GAWM, s vah-RYEN^y-yem).
Tarts (filled with fish, cottage cheese, or jam).

858. Пирог (с мясом, с рыбой, с капустой, с рисом и грибами).
p^{y}ee-RAWK (s MYAH-sum, s RIH-boў, s kah-POOS-toў, s R^{y}EE-sum ee gr^{y}ee-BAH-m^{y}ee).
Two layers of yeast dough (filled with meat or fish, sauerkraut, rice and mushrooms, and a variety of other stuffing).

859. Пирог сладкий (с яблоками, с абрикосами, со сливами, с вишнями).
p^{y}ee-RAWK SLAHT-k^{y}ee‿ў (s YAHB-luh-kah-m^{y}ee, s ah-br^{y}ee-KAW-sah-m^{y}ee, sah SL^{y}EE-vah-m^{y}ee s V^{y}EESH-nyah-m^{y}ee).
Sweet pie (with fruit or jam filling, apples, apricots, plums, cherries).

860. Пирожки (с мясом, с капустой, с морковью, с вишнями).
p^{y}ee-rahsh-K^{y}EE (s MYAH-sum, s kah-POOS-toў, s mahr-KAWV^y-yoo s V^{y}EESH-nyah-m^{y}ee).
Small pies of yeast dough (stuffed with meat, sauerkraut, carrots, or cherries).

861. Пирожки слоёные.
p^{y}ee-rahsh-K^{y}EE slah-YAW-nih-yeh.
Flake dough pastry (stuffed with various fillings usually served with soup).

862. Хлеб белый (пшеничный).
khlyep BYEH-lih‿ў (psheh-N^{y}EECH-nih‿ў).
White (wheat) bread.

863. Хлеб чёрный (ржаной).
khlyep CHAWR-nih‿ў (rzhah-NOЎ).
Dark (rye) bread.

864. Хлеб пеклеванный.
khlyep pyek-lyeh-VAHN-nih‿ў.
Pumpernickel bread.

SOUPS

865. Борщ.
bawrshch.
Borsht (red beet vegetable soup).

866. Ботвинья.
baht-VʸEENʸ-yah.
Fish and vegetable soup.

867. Бульон с клёцками.
boolʸ-YAWN(s KLYAWTS-kah-mʸee).
Clear soup (with dumplings).

868. Куриный суп.
koo-RʸEE-nih‿ў soop.
Chicken soup.

869. Окрошка.
ahk-RAWSH-kah.
Cold soup (made of hash and kvass).

870. Рассольник с почками.
rahs-SAWLʸ-nʸeek s PAWCH-kah-mʸee.
Kidney soup with pickled cucumbers.

871. Солянка (мясная) рыбная.
sah-LYAHN-kah (myahs-NAH-yah) RIHB-nah-yah.
Thick sauerkraut and (meat) fish soup.

872. Суп из овощей.
soop eez uh-vah-SHCHEʸ.
Vegetable soup.

873. Суп картофельный.
soop kahr-TAW-fyelʸ-nih‿ў.
Potato soup.

874. Суп с вермишелью.
soop s vyehr-m^{y}ee-SHEL^y-yoo.
Vermicelli soup.

875. Суп-пюре из помидор.
soop pyoo-REH eez puh-m^{y}ee-DAWR.
Cream of tomato soup.

876. Уха.
oo-KHAH.
Clear fish soup.

877. Щи.
shchee.
Cabbage or sauerkraut soup.

878. Щи зелёные.
shchee zyeh-LYAW-nih-yeh.
Spinach soup (served with sour cream and hard
boiled eggs).

FISH

879. Битки из рыбы.
b^{y}eet-K^{y}EE eez RIH-bih.
Fish balls.

880. Камбала в красном вине.
kahm-bah-LAH f KRAS-num v^{y}ee-NYEH.
Flounder in red wine.

881. Карп жареный.
kahrp ZHAH-ryeh-nih⌣ў.
Fried carp.

882. Крабы.
KRAH-bih.
Crabs.

883. Лещ фаршированный кашей.
lyeshch fahr-shee-RAW-vahn-nih⌣ў KAH-sheў.
Bream stuffed with buckwheat.

884. Осетрина паровая.
uh-syet-R^{y}EE-nah pah-rah-VAH-yah.
Sturgeon cooked over steam.

885. Раки.
RAH-k^{y}ee.
Crawfish.

886. Сазан запечёный.
sah-ZAHN zah-pyeh-CHAW-nih‿y̌.
Baked carp.

887. Севрюга в томате.
syev-RYOO-gah f tah-MAH-tyeh.
Sturgeon in tomato sauce.

888. Стерлядь "кольчиком".
STYEHR-lyaht^y "KAWL^y-chee-kum".
Young sturgeon boiled in a "ring".

889. Судак отварной.
soo-DAHK ut-vahr-NOY̌.
Boiled pike.

890. Угорь (копчёный).
OO-gawr^y (kahp-CHAW-nih‿y̌).
Eel (smoked).

891. Щука фаршированная.
SHCHOO-kah fahr-shee-RAW-vahn-nah-yah.
Pickerel (stuffed with ground, seasoned fish meat).

MEAT

892. Баранья ножка жареная.
bah-RAHN^y-yah NAWSH-kah ZHAH-ryeh-nah-yah.
Roast leg of lamb.

893. Беф строганов.
byef STRAW-gah-nuf.
Beef Stroganov (small pieces of beef with mushrooms, onions and a sour cream sauce).

894. Биточки.
b^yee-TAWCH-k^yee.
Meat balls, flat, small size.

895. Ветчина жареная.
vyeh-chee-NAH ZHAH-ryeh-nah-yah.
Roast ham.

896. Голубцы.
guh-loop-TSIH.
Stuffed cabbage rolls.

897. Гуляш.
goo-LYAHSH.
Hungarian goulash.

898. Зразы.
ZRAH-zih.
Meat rolls stuffed with buckwheat gruel or rice.

899. Котлеты отбивные.
kaht-LYEH-tih ut-b^yeev-NIH-yeh.
Chops (any variety).

900. Котлеты с макаронами.
kaht-LYEH-tih s mah-kah-RAW-nah-m^yee.
Large meat balls with macaroni.

901. Мозги жареные.
mahz-G^yEE ZHAH-ryeh-nih-yeh.
Fried brains.

902. Мясная запеканка.
myahs-NAH-yah zah-pyeh-KAHN-kah.
Meat loaf.

903. Пельмени по-сибирски.
pyel^y-MYEH-n^yee puh-s^yee-B^yEER-sk^yee.
Meat filled dumplings (frozen, cooked and served
in its own broth).

904. Плов (пилав из баранины).
plawf (p^yee-LAHF eez bah-RAH-n^yee-nih).
Mutton (with rice, raisins and plums).

905. Поросёнок жареный.
puh-rah-SYAW-nuk ZHAH-ryeh-nih_y̆.
Roast suckling pig.

906. Почки в вине.
PAWCH-k^yee v v^yee-NYEH.
Kidneys in wine.

907. Рагу мясное.
rah-GOO myahs-NAW-yeh.
Meat stew.

908. Рулет мясной.
roo-LYET myahs-NOY̆.
Beef roll.

909. Свиные отбивные.
sv^yee-NIH-yeh ut-b^yeev-NIH-yeh.
Pork chops.

910. Студень (свиной) телячий.
STOO-dyen^y (sv^yee-NOY̆) tyeh-LYAH-chee_y̆.
Jellied veal (pork).

911. Тефтели в томате.
TYEF-tyeh-l^yee f tah-MAH-tyeh.
Very small meat balls in tomato sauce.

912. Телятина жареная.
tyeh-LYAH-t^yee-nah ZHAH-ryeh-nah-yah.
Roast veal.

913. Тушёное мясо.
too-SHAW-nuh-yeh MYAH-suh.
Pot roast.

914. Шашлык.
shahsh-LIHK.
Small pieces of lamb fried over open fire on a spit.

915. Шницель.
SHN^{y}EE-tsel^y.
Breaded veal or pork chop.

POULTRY

916. Гусь с кислой капустой.
goos^y s K^{y}EES-loў kah-POOS-toў.
Roast goose with sauerkraut stuffing.

917. Индейка жареная фаршированная кашта-
нами.
een-DYEЎ-kah ZHAH-ryeh-nah-yah fahr-shee-RAW-vahn-nah-yah kahsh-TAH-nah-m^{y}ee.
Roast turkey with chestnut stuffing.

918. Котлеты пожарские.
kaht-LYEH-tih pah-ZHAHR-sk^{y}ee-yeh.
Chicken patties.

919. Курица отварная под белым соусом.
KOO-r^{y}ee-tsah ut-vahr-NAH-yah paht BYEH-lihm SAW-oo-sum.
Boiled chicken with white sauce.

920. Утка с яблоками.
OOT-kah s YAHB-luh-kah-m^{y}ee.
Roast duck with apple stuffing.

GAME

921. Вальдшнеп.
vahl^{y}d-SHNYEP.
Woodcock.

922. Заяц в сметане.
ZAH-yahts f smyeh-TAH-nyeh.
Roast hare in sour cream sauce.

923. Заяц фаршированный.
ZAH-yahts fahr-shee-RAW-vahn-nih‿ў.
Stuffed hare.

924. Кролик в белом соусе.
KRAW-l^{y}eek f BYEH-lum SAW-oo-syeh.
Rabbit in white sauce.

925. Куропатка жареная.
koo-rah-PAHT-kah ZHAH-ryeh-nah-yah.
Roast partridge.

926. Перепел жареный.
PYEH-ryeh-pyel ZHAH-ryeh-nih‿ў.
Roast quail.

927. Рябчики жареные.
RYAHP-chee-k^{y}ee ZHAH-ryeh-nih-yeh.
Roast grouse.

VEGETABLES: VEGETABLE DISHES

928. Артишоки отварные.
ahr-t^{y}ee-SHAW-k^{y}ee ut-vahr-NIH-yeh.
Boiled artichokes.

929. Баклажаны жареные.
bahk-lah-ZHAH-nih ZHAH-ryeh-nih-yeh.
Fried eggplants.

930. Баклажаны тушёные в сметане.
bahk-lah-ZHAH-nih too-SHAW-nih-yeh f smyeh-TAH-nyeh.
Eggplants stewed in sour cream.

931. Баклажаны фаршированные (мясом) овощами.
bahk-lah-ZHAH-nih fahr-shee-RAW-vahn-nih-yeh (MYAH-sum) uh-vah-SHCHAH-m^{y}ee.
Eggplants stuffed with (meat) vegetables.

932. Голубцы (мясные) овощные.
guh-loop-TSIH (myahs-NIH-yeh) uh-vahshch-NIH-yeh.
Cabbage leaves stuffed with (meat) vegetables.

933. Гречневая каша.
GRYESH-nyeh-vah KAH-shah.
Buckwheat groats.

934. Зелёный горошек в масле.
zyeh-LYAW-nih_ў gah-RAW-shek v MAHS-lyeh.
Buttered green peas.

935. Кабачки жареные.
kah-bahch-K^{y}EE ZHAH-ryeh-nih-yeh.
Fried squash.

936. Кабачки фаршированные (мясом) рисом.
kah-bahch-K^{y}EE fahr-shee-RAW-vahn-nih-yeh (MYAH-sum) R^{y}EE-sum.
Squash stuffed with (meat) rice.

937. Капуста цветная с сухарями.
kah-POOS-tah tsvyet-NAH-yah s soo-khah-RYAH-m^{y}ee.
Cauliflower with buttered bread crumbs.

938. Капуста брюссельская в молочном соусе.
kah-POOS-tah BRYOOS-syel^y-skah-yah v mah-LAWCH-num SAW-oo-syeh.
Brussels sprouts in milk sauce.

939. Картофель в сметане.
kahr-TAW-fyel^y f smyeh-TAH-nyeh.
Potatoes in sour cream.

940. Кислая капуста.
K^{y}EES-lah-yah kah-POOS-tah.
Sauerkraut.

941. Котлеты капусные.
kaht-LYEH-tih kah-POOS-nih-yeh.
Chopped cabbage patties.

942. Кукуруза в початках.
koo-koo-ROO-zah f pah-CHAHT-kahkh.
Corn on cob.

943. Перец фаршированный (мясом) овощами.
PYEH-ryets fahr-shee-RAW-vahn-nih‿ў (MYAH-sum) uh-vah-SHCHAH-m^{y}ee.
Green peppers stuffed with (meat) vegetables.

944. Помидоры фаршированные мясом.
puh-m^{y}ee-DAW-rih fahr-shee-RAW-vahn-nıh-yeh MYAH-sum.
Tomatoes stuffed with meat.

945. Рагу из овощей.
rah-GOO eez uh-vah-SHCHEЎ.
Vegetable stew.

946. Редиска со сметаной.
ryeh-D^{y}EES-keh sah smyeh-TAH-nuh‿ў.
Radish with sour cream.

947. Тыква под молочным соусом.
TIHK-vah pud mah-LAWCH-nihm SAW-oo-sum.
Pumpkin in milk sauce.

948. Щавель.
shchah-VYEL^y.
Sorrel.

SALADS

949. Салат из дичи.
sah-LAHT eez D^{y}EE-chee.
Game salad.

950. Салат из капусты.
sah-LAHT ees kah-POOS-tih.
Cabbage salad.

951. Салат из квашеной капусты.
sah-LAHT ees KVAH-sheh-nuh‿ў kah-POOS-tih.
Sauerkraut salad.

952. Салат из мяса.
sah-LAHT eez MYAH-sah.
Meat salad.

953. Салат картофельный.
sah-LAHT kahr-TAW-fyelʸ-nih‿ў.
Potato salad.

954. Салат из свёклы.
sah-LAHT ees SVYAWK-lih.
Red beet salad.

955. Салат из свежих помидор и огурцов.
*sah-LAHT ees SVYEH-zheekh puh-mʸee-DAWR
ee uh-goor-TSAWF.*
Tomato and cucumber salad.

956. Салат из фруктов.
sah-LAHT ees FROOK-tuf.
Fruit salad.

957. Салат со сметаной и яйцом.
*sah-LAHT suh smyeh-TAH-nuh‿ў ee yah‿ў-
TSAWM.*
Mixed salad with boiled eggs and sour cream.

958. Винигрет.
vʸee-nʸee-GRYET.
Mixed salad (of boiled carrots, red beets, beans,
potatoes, pickled cucumbers, and onions, with
vinegar and salad oil).

DESSERTS

959. Блинчики с вареньем.
BLʸEEN-chee-kee s vah-RYENʸ-yem.
Thin pancakes with jam.

960. Блины.
bl^{y}ee-NIH.
Pancakes.

961. Варенники с творогом.
vah-RYEN-n^{y}ee-k^{y}ee s tvuh-rah-GAWM.
Cheese dumplings.

962. Ватрушка.
vah-TROOSH-kah.
Cheese tart.

963. Желе.
zheh-LYEH.
Jello.

964. Кекс английский.
kyeks ahn-GL^{y}EE⌣Ĭ-sk^{y}ee⌣ў.
English cake (pound cake).

965. Кисель.
kee-SYEL^y.
Jello dessert (made of fruit juice thickened with
potato starch).

966. Компот.
kahm-PAWT.
Stewed fruit.

967. Конфекты.
kahn-FYEH-tih.
Candies.

968. Мороженое.
mah-RAW-zheh-nuh-yeh.
Ice cream.

969. земляничное.   *zyem-lyah-N^{y}EECH-nuh-yeh.*
Strawberry.

970. сливочное.   *SL^{y}EE-vuch-nuh-yeh.*   Vanilla.

971. шоколадное. *shuh-kah-LAHT-nuh-yeh.*
Chocolate.

972. ореховое. *ah-RYEH-khuh-vuh-yeh.* Nut.

973. Мусс из ягод.
moos eez YAH-guht.
Mousse (made with whipped fruit juice).

974. Пастила.
pah-st^yee-LAH.
Candied fruit paste (native candy of Moscow).

975. Печенье.
pyeh-CHEN^y-yeh.
Cookies.

976. Пирожные.
p^yee-RAWZH-nih-yeh.
Small cakes.

977. Повидло.
pah-V^yEED-luh.
Fruit butter.

978. Пудинг.
POO-d^yeeng.
Pudding.

979. Рулет бисквитный.
roo-LYET b^yee-SKV^yEET-nih‿y̆.
Sponge roll.

980. Сливки сбитые.
SL^yEEV-k^yee SB^yEE-tih-yeh.
Whipped cream.

981. Торт.
tawrt.
Cake (usually layer cake).

982. Бисквитный торт.
b^yee-SKV^yEET-nih‿ў tawrt.
Sponge cake.

983. "Наполеон" торт.
nah-puh-lyeh-AWN tawrt.
"Napoleon" cake (made of flake dough and custard).

984. Песочный торт.
pyeh-SAWCH-nih‿ў tawrt.
Short cake.

985. Творожники.
tvah-RAWZH-n^yee-k^yee.
Cottage cheese fritters (served with melted butter and sour cream).

986. Шарлотка.
shahr-LAWT-kah.
Charlotte.

987. Шоколадный крем.
shuh-kuh-LAHD-nih‿ў kryem.
Chocolate pudding.

988. Яблоки печёные.
YAHB-luh-k^yee pyeh-CHAW-nih-yeh.
Baked apples.

989. Яблоки в слойке.
YAHB-luh-k^yee f SLOЎ-kyeh.
Apple turnover.

990. Яблоки в тесте.
YAHB-luh-k^yee f TYES-tyeh.
Apple dumpling.

991. Сыр.
sihr.
Cheese.

992. Голландский сыр.
   'gahl-LAHN-sk^{y}ee‿ў sihr.
   Dutch cheese.

993. Советский сыр.
   sah-VYET-sk^{y}ee‿ў sihr.
   Soviet cheese.

994. Рокфор сыр.
   rahk-FAWR sihr..
   Roquefort.

995. Швейцарский сыр.
   SHVYEЎ-tsahr-sk^{y}eeў sihr.
   Swiss cheese.

996. Студень из головы.
   STOO-dyen^y eez guh-LAW-vih.
   Head cheese.

997. Сырок чайный.
   sih-RAWK CHAH‿Ў-nih‿ў.
   Sweet cream cheese with candied fruit.

998. Творог.
   tvah-RAWK.
   Cottage cheese.

BEVERAGES

999. Боржом.
   bahr-ZHAWM.
   "Borzhom" (mineral waters).

1000. Газированная вода (с сиропом).
   gah-z^{y}ee-RAW-vahn-nah-yah vah-DAH (s s^{y}ee-
     RAW-pum).
   Soda water (with fruit syrup).

1001. Какао.
   kah-KAH-aw.
   Cocoa.

1002. Квас.
kvahs.
Mild beer-like beverage.

1003. Кефир.
kyeh-F^{y}EER.
Fermented milk.

1004. Кофе.
KAW-fyeh.
Coffee.

1005. Лимонад.
l^{y}ee-mah-NAHT.
Lemonade.

1006. Минеральная вода.
myee-nyeh-RAHL^y-nah-yah vah-DAH.
Mineral water.

1007. Молоко.
muh-lah-KAW.
Milk.

1008. Оранжад.
uh-rahn-ZHANT.
Orange drink.

1009. Чай.
chah‿ў.
Tea.

1010. Шоколад.
shuh-kah-LAHT.
Chocolate (drink).

APPENDIX II (not recorded)
MISCELLANEOUS ARTICLES

1011. Artists' supplies.
Материалы для художников.
mah-tyeh-RYAH-lih dlyah khoo-DAWZH-n^{y}ee-kuf.

1012. Ash trays.
Пепельницы.
PYEH-pyelʸ-nʸee-tsih.

1013. Boxed candies.
Конфекты в коробках.
kahn-FYEH-tih f kah-RAWP-kahkh.

1014. Playing cards.
Карты.
KAHR-tih.

1015. Chess set.
Шахматы.
SHAHKH-mah-tih.

1016. China.
Фарфор.
fahr-FAWR.

1017. Silver compacts.
Серебряные пудреницы.
syeh-RYEB-ryeh-nih-yeh POOD-ryeh-nʸee-tsih.

1018. Gold cuff links.
золотые запонки.
zuh-lah-TIH-yeh ZAH-pun-kʸee.

1019. Dolls.
Куклы.
KOOK-lih.

1020. Earrings.
Серьги.
SYEHRʸ-gʸee.

1021. Embroidery.
Вышивки.
VIH-sheef-kʸee.

1022. Russian lace.
Русские кружева.
ROOS-kʸee-yeh kroo-zheh-VAH.

1023. Sheet music.
Ноты.
NAW-tih.

1024. Musical instruments.
Музыкальные инструменты.
moo-zih-KAHL^y-nih-yeh een-stroo-MYEN-tih.

1025. Perfume.
Духи.
doo-KH^yEE.

1026. Pictures.
Картины.
kahr-T^yEE-nih.

1027. Tea pot cozies.
Грелки на чайник.
GRYEL-k^yee nah CHAH‿Ĭ-n^yeek.

1028. Radio sets.
Радио аппараты.
RAH-d^yee-aw ah-pah-RAHT-tih.

1029. Television sets.
Телевизоры.
tyeh-lyeh-V^yEE-zuh-rih.

1030. Records.
Пластинки.
plah-ST^yEEN-k^yee.

1031. Pottery.
Глиняные изделия.
GL^yEE-nyeh-nih-yeh eez-DYEH-l^yee-yah.

1032. Antique silverware.
Старинное серебро.
stah-R^yEEN-nuh-yeh syeh-ryeh-BRAW.

1033. Toys.
Игрушки.
ee-GROOSH-k^yee.

1034. Woodwork of Russian workmanship.
Деревянные изделия русской работы.
dyeh-ryeh-VYAHN-nih-yeh ee-DYEL^y-yah ROO-skuh‿ў rah-BAW-tih.

1035. Souvenirs.
Сувениры.
soo-vyeh-N^yEE-rih.

1036. Silk umbrellas.
Шёлковые зонтики.
SHAWL-kuh-vih-yeh ZAWN-t^yee-k^yee.

1037. Wrist watches.
Часы на руку.
chah-SIH nah ROO-koo.

APPENDIX III (not recorded)
DRUGS AND COSMETICS

1038. Adhesive tape. Липкий пластырь.
L^yEEP-k^yee‿ў PLAH-stihr^y.

1039. Alcohol. Спирт. *sp^yeert.*

1040. Antiseptic. Антисептическое средство.
ahn-t^yee-syep-T^yEE-cheh-skuh-yeh SRYET-svuh.

1041. Bandage. Бинт. *b^yeent.*

1042. Bicarbonate of soda. Сода. *SAW-dah.*

1043. Bobby pins. Заколки для волос.
zah-KAWL-k^yee dlyah vah-LAWS.

1044. Boric acid. Борная кислота.
BAWR-nah-yah k^yees-lah-TAH.

1045. Cleaning fluid.
Жидкость для вывода пятен.
ZHEET-kust^y dlyah BIH-vuh-dah PYAH-tyen.

1046. Cold cream. Кольдкрем. *kawl^yt-krem.*

1047. Cologne. Одеколон. *AW-deh-kah-LAWN.*

1048. Comb. Гребёнка. *gryeh-BYAWN-kah.*

1049. Compact. Пудреница. *POOD-ryeh-n^yee-tsah.*

1050. Corn pads. Мозольный пластырь.
mah-ZAWL^y-nih_ў PLAH-stihr^y.

1051. Cotton. Вата. *VAH-tah.*

1052. Depilatory. Средство для удаления волос.
*SRYET-stvuh dlyah oo-dah-LYEH-n^yee-yah vah-
LAWS.*

1053. Epsom salts. Английская соль.
ahn-GL^yEE_Ў-skah-yah sawl^y.

1054. Gauze. Марля. *MAHR-lyah.*

1055. Hairbrush. Щётка для волос.
SHCHAWT-kah dlyah vah-LAWS.

1056. Hair clips. Приколки для волос.
pr^yee-KAWL-k^yee dlyah vah-LAWS.

1057. Hair net. Сетка для волос.
SYET-kah dlyah vah-LAWS.

1058. Hair pins. Шпильки. *SHP^yEEL^y-k^yee.*

1059. Hot water bottle. Грелка. *GRYEL-kah.*

1060. Ice bag. Пузырь для льда.
poo-ZIHR^y dlyah l^y-dah.

1061. Insecticide.
Средство для истребления насекомых.
SRYET-stvuh dlyah ees-tryeb-LYEH-n^yee-yah nah-syeh-KAW-mihkh.

1062. Iodine.   Иод.   *ee-AWT.*

1063. Laxative (mild).
Слабительное (не сильно-действующее).
slah-B^yEE-tyel^y-nuh-yeh (nyeh S^yEEL^y-nuh DYEY-stvoo-yoo-shcheh-yeh).

1064. Lipstick.   Губная помада.
goob-NAH-yah pah-MAH-dah.

1065. Medicine dropper.
Пипетка.
p^yee-PYET-kah.

1066. Mirror.   Зеркало.   *ZYEHR-kah-luh.*

1067. Mouth wash.   Полосканье для рта.
puh-lah-SKAHN^y-yeh dlyah rtah.

1068. Nail file.   Пилка для ногтей.
P^yEEL-kah dlyah nahk-TYEY.

1069. Nail polish.   Лак для ногтей.
lahk dlyah nahk-TYEY.

1070. Nail polish remover.
Средство для удаления лака.
SRYET-stvuh dlyah oo-dah-LYEH-n^yee-yah LAH-kah.

1071. Peroxide.   Перекись водорода.
PYEH-r^yee-k^yees^y vuh-dah-RAW-dah.

1072. Pins.   Булавки.   *boo-LAHF-k^yee.*

1073. Powder.   Порошок.   *puh-rah-SHAWK.*

1074. Face powder. Пудра. *POOD-rah.*

1075. Foot powder. Порошок для ног.
puh-rah-SHAWK dlyah nawk.

1076. Talcum powder. Тальк в порошке.
tahl^{y}k f puh-rah-SHKΥEN.

1077. Razor. Бритва. *BR^{y}EET-vah.*

1078. Electric razor. Электрическая бритва.
eh-lyeh-TR^{y}EE-cheh-skah-yah BR^{y}EET-vah.

1079. Razor blades. Лезвия для бритвы.
LYEZ-v^{y}ee-yah dlyah BR^{y}EET-vih.

1080. Rouge. Румяна. *roo-MYAH-nah.*

1081. Safety pins. Английские булавки.
ahn-GL^{y}EE_$\Ymath$-sk^{y}ee-yeh boo-LAHF-k^{y}ee.

1082. Scissors. Ножницы. *NAWZH-n^{y}ee-tsih.*

1083. Sedative. Успокаивающее средство.
oo-spah-KAH-^{y}ee-vah-yoo-shcheh-yeh SRΥET-stvuh.

1084. Shampoo. Шампунь. *shahm-POON^y.*

1085. Shaving cream. Крем для бритья.
kryem dlyah br^{y}eet^y-ΥAH.

1086. Smelling salts. Нюхательная соль.
NΥOO-khah-tyel^y-nah-yah sawl^y.

1087. Soap. Мыло. *MIH-luh.*

1088. Sponge. Губка. *GOOP-kah.*

1089. Stopper (bath or sink). Пробка.
PRAWP-kah.

1090. Sunburn ointment.
Мазь от солнечного ожога.
mahz^y aht SAWL-nyech-nuh-vuh ah-ZHAW-gah.

1091. **Sunglasses.** Солнечные очки.
SAWL-nyech-nih-yeh ahch-K^{y}EE.

1092. **Suntan oil.** Мазь для загара.
mahz^y dlyah zah-GAH-rah.

1093. **Thermometer.** Термометр.
tyehr-MAW-myetr.

1094. **Toothbrush.** Зубная щётка.
zoob-NAH-yah SHCHAWT-kah.

1095. **Toothpaste.** Зубная паста.
zoob-NAH-yah PAHS-tah.

1096. **Toothpowder.** Зубной порошок.
zoob-NOҮ puh-rah-SHAWK.

1097. **Vaseline.** Вазелин. *vah-zyeh-L^{y}EEN.*

1098. **Washcloth.** Мочалка. *mah-CHAHL-kah.*

1099. **Zipper.** Застёжка-молния.
zah-STYAWSH-kah-MAWL-n^{y}ee-yah.

APPENDIX IV (not recorded)
PARTS OF THE CAR

1100. **Accelerator.** Акселератор.
ahk-syeh-lyeh-RAH-tur.

1101. **Air filter.** Очиститель воздуха.
uh-chee-ST^{y}EE-tyel^y VAWZ-doo-khah.

1102. **Axle.** Ось. *aws^y.*

1103. **Battery.** Батарея. *bah-tah-RYEH-yah.*

1104. **Body** (of car). Кузов. *KOO-zuf.*

1105. Brake. Тормоз. *TAWR-mus.*

1106. Emergency brake. Запасной тормоз.
zah-pahs-NOY̆ TAWR-mus.

1107. Foot brake. Ножной тормоз.
nahzh-NOY̆ TAWR-mus.

1108. Hand brake. Ручной тормоз.
rooch-NOY̆ TAWR-mus.

1109. Bumper. Буфер. *BOO-fyehr.*

1110. Carburetor. Карбюратор.
kahr-byoo-RAH-tur.

1111. Choke. Дроссель. *DRAWS-syel^y.*

1112. Clutch. Сцепление. *stseh-PLYEH-n^{y}ee-yeh.*

1113. Cylinder. Цилиндр. *tsee-L^{y}EENDR.*

1114. Differential. Дифференциал.
d^{y}eef-fyeh-ryen-tsee-AHL.

1115. Directional signal. Сигнальная лампа.
s^{y}eeg-NAHL^y-nah-yah LAHM-pah.

1116. Door. Дверь. *dvyehr^y.*

1117. Electrical system. Электрическая система.
eh-lyek-TR^{y}EE-cheh-skah-yah s^{y}ees-TYEH-mah.

1118. Engine. Мотор. *mah-TAWR.*

1119. Exhaust pipe. Выхлопная трубка.
vih-khlahp-NAH-yah TROOP-kah.

1120. Fan (ventilator). Вентилятор.
vyen-t^{y}ee-LYAH-tur.

1121. Fan belt. Ремень вентилятора.
ryeh-MYEN^y vyen-t^{y}ee-LYAH-tuh-rah.

1122. **Fender.** Крыло. *krih-LAW.*

1123. **Fuel pump.** Топливопровод.
TAWP-l^{y}ee-vuh-pruh-VAWT.

1124. **Fuse.** Предохранитель.
pryeh-duh-khrah-N^{y}EE-tyel^y.

1125. **Gear shift.**
Механизм переключения передач.
myeh-khah-N^{y}EEZM pyeh-ryeh-klyoo-CHEN-n^{y}ee-
yah pyeh-ryeh-DAHCH.

1126. **Generator.** Генератор. *gyeh-nyeh-RAH-tur.*

1127. **Heater.** Отопитель. *uh-tah-P^{y}EE-tyel^y.*

1128. **Hood.** Капот. *kah-PAWT.*

1129. **Horn.** Рожок. *rah-ZHAWK.*

1130. **Ignition.** Зажигание. *zah-zhee-GAH-n^{y}ee-yeh.*

1131. **License plate.** Табличка с номером.
tahb-L^{y}EECH-kah s NAW-myeh-rum.

1132. **Light.** Свет. *svyet.*

1133. **Head lights.** Фары. *FAH-rih.*

1134. **Parking light.** Сигнал стоянки.
s^{y}eeg-NAHL stah-YAHN-k^{y}ee.

1135. **Stop light.** Остановочный свет.
uh-stah-NAW-vuch-nih_ў svyet.

1136. **Tail light.** Задний свет. *ZAHD-n^{y}ee_ў svyet.*

1137. **Lubrication system.** Смазочная система.
SMAH-zuch-nah-yah s^{y}ees-TYEH-mah.

1138. **Motor.** Мотор. *mah-TAWR.*

1139. **Muffler.** Глушитель. *gloo-SHEE-tyel^y.*

1140. Nut. Гайка. *GAH‿ Y̆-kah.*

1141. Radiator. Радиатор. *rah-d^yee-AH-tur.*

1142. Radio. Радио. *RAH-d^yee-aw.*

1143. Automatic shift.
Автоматическая передача.
ahf-tuh-mah-T^yEE-cheh-skah-yah   pyeh-ryeh-DAH-chah.

1144. Reverse shift. Задняя передача.
ZAHD-nyah-yah pyeh-ryeh-DAH-chah.

1145. Shock absorber. Амортизатор.
ah-mur-t^yee-ZAH-tur.

1146. Spark plugs. Свечи. *SVYEH-chee.*

1147. Spring. Рессора. *ryeh-SAW-rah.*

1148. Starter. Стартер. *STAHR-tyehr.*

1149. Steering wheel. Колесо управления.
kuh-lyeh-SAW oo-prahv-LYEH-n^yee-yah.

1150. Tank. Бак. *bahk.*

1151. Tire. Шина. *SHEE-nah.*

1152. Spare tire. Запасная шина.
zah-pahs-NAH-yah SHEE-nah.

1153. Transmission. Передача.
pyeh-ryeh-DAH-chah.

1154. Trunk. Багажник. *bah-GAHZH-n^yeek.*

1155. Valve. Клапан. *KLAH-pahn.*

1156. Water cooling system.
Водяное охлаждение.
vuh-dyah-NAW-yeh uhkh-lahzh-DYEH-n^yee-yeh.

1157. Wheel. Колесо. *kuh-lyeh-SAW.*

1158. **Front wheel.** Переднее колесо.
pyeh-RYED-nyeh-yeh kuh-lyeh-SAW.

1159. **Rear wheel.** Заднее колесо.
ZAHD-nyeh-yeh kuh-lyeh-SAW.

1160. **Windshield wiper.** Стеклоочиститель.
STYEK-luh-uh-chee-STᵞEE-tyelᵞ.

APPENDIX V (not recorded)
TOOLS AND ACCESSORIES

1161. **Alcohol.** Спирт. *spᵞeert.*

1162. **Anti-freeze.** Антифриз. *ahn-tᵞee-FRᵞEES.*

1163. **Bolt.** Болт. *bawlt.*

1164. **Bulb.** Лампочка. *LAHM-puch-kah.*

1165. **Chains.** Цепи. *TSEH-pᵞee.*

1166. **Flashlight.** Карманный фонарик.
kahr-MAHN-nih⌣y̆ fah-NAH-rᵞeek.

1167. **Grease.** Тавот. *tah-VAWT.*

1168. **Hammer.** Молоток. *muh-lah-TAWK.*

1169. **Jack.** Домкрат. *dahm-KRAHT.*

1170. **Key.** Ключ. *klyooch.*

1171. **Nail.** Гвоздь. *gvawztᵞ.*

1172. **Nut.** Гайка. *GAH⌣Y̆-kah.*

1173. **Oil.** Жидкое масло.
ZHEET-kuh-yeh MAHS-luh.

1174. **Pliers.** Плоскогубцы.
PLAWS-kuh-GOOP-tsih.

1175. Rags. Тряпки. *TRYAHP-k^yee.*

1176. Rope. Верёвка. *vyeh-RYAWF-kah.*

1177. Screw. Винт. *v^yeent.*

1178. Screwdriver. Отвёртка. *aht-VYAWRT-kah.*

1179. Skid chains. Цепь против скольжения.
　　tsyep^y PRAW-t^yeef skahl^y-ZHEH-n^yee-yah.

1180. Tire pump. Насос для шин.
　　nah-SAWS dlyah sh^yeen.

1181. Tools. Инструменты. *een-stroo-MYEN-tih.*

1182. Wrench. Гаечный ключ.
　　GAH-yech-nih‿y̌ klyooch.

SIGNS AND PUBLIC NOTICES

(The following list of signs and notices is not recorded. For your convenience, these lists have been alphabetized in Russian.)

This list includes most of the recurring signs and notices that one sees on the streets and public places of a city. There is no need to memorize this list but do review it when you arrive in the country. If you plan to drive, the study of road signs is, of course, imperative. With the help of this list or a pocket dictionary, make an effort to learn the meaning of common signs you see. It is an excellent way to build your vocabulary in the course of your travels because signs and notices, by and large, reflect the current language that answers everyday practical needs. You will also find that when you understand almost all the common signs you see around you, you will be more at home and confident in your new environment.

APPENDIX VI (not recorded)
ROAD SIGNS

1183. Автомобильная езда воспрещается.
Automobiles prohibited.

1184. Берегись (поезда) трамвая.
Beware of the (train) streetcar.

1185. Бензоколонка.
Gasoline pump.

1186. Больница.
Hospital.

1187. Бюро справок.
Information bureau.

1188. В.
To (a destination).

1189. Велосипед.
Bicycle.

1190. Впереди крутой поворот.
Sharp turn ahead.

1191. Военная зона.
Military zone.

1192. Въезд.
Entrance.

1193. Выезд.
Exit.

1194. Граница.
Border.

1195. Грузовик.
Truck.

1196. Грузовое движение воспрещается.
Heavy traffic prohibited.

1197. Грунтовая дорога.
Dirt road.

1198. Движение в одном направлении.
One-way traffic.

1199. Движение закрыто.
Closed to traffic.

1200. Двойной поворот.
Double curve.

1201. Держись (правой) левой стороны.
Keep to the (right) left.

1202. Дом отдыха.
Rest home.

1203. Дорога в плохом состоянии.
Road in bad condition.

1204. Дорога закрыта.
Road closed.

1205. Дорога ремонтируется.
Road under repair.

1206. Езда на (велосипедах) мотоциклах воспрещается.
(Bicycles) motorcycles prohibited.

1207. Железнодорожный переезд.
Railroad crossing.

1208. Закрыто.
Closed.

1209. Замедлить ход.
Slow down.

1210. Заправочный пункт.
Gas station.

1211. Извилистая дорога.
Winding road.

1212. Конец мощёной дороги.
End of paved road.

1213. Крутой (спуск) под'ем.
Steep (dip) grade.

1214. Курить воспрещается.
Smoking prohibited.

1215. Легковая машина.
Passenger car.

1216. Легковой автомобиль.
Passenger car.

1217. Медленная езда.
Drive slowly.

1218. Медпункт.
First aid station.

1219. Мост.
Bridge.

1220. Мотоцикл.
Motorcycle.

1221. Налево.
To the left.

1222. Направо.
To the right.

1223. Нет движения.
Closed to traffic.

1224. Нет проезда.
No thoroughfare.

1225. Нет стоянки.
No parking.

1226. Обгон воспрещается.
Overtaking prohibited.

1227. Область.
Province (administrative unit).

1228. Объезд.
Detour.

1229. Опасно.
Dangerous.

1230. Опасный поворот.
Dangerous curve.

1231. Остановка (автобуса) трамвая.
(Bus) streetcar stop.

1232. Осторожно.
Look out.

1233. Осторожно, пешеходы.
Careful, pedestrians.

1234. Паром.
Ferry.

1235. Перекрёсток.
Crossroads, streetcrossing, intersection.

1236. Пересечение дорог.
Road crossing.

1237. Пешеходы.
Pedestrians.

1238. Площадь.
Square.

1239. Поворот.
Turn.

1240. Поворот (направо) налево.
Turn (right) left.

1241. Поворот (направо) налево воспрещается.
No (right) left turn.

1242. Полный ход.
Resume speed.

1243. Предельная скорость . . . км в час.
Speed limit . . . kilometers per hour.

1244. Предельный груз.
Load limit.

1245. Предельная тяжесть.
Weight limit.

1246. Предельная (ширина) высота.
Height (width) limit.

1247. Провода высокого напряжения.
High tension wires.

1248. Проезд в одну сторону.
One-way traffic.

1249. Проезд воспрещается.
Road closed.

1250. Проезд закрыт.
No thoroughfare.

1251. Пункт скорой помощи.
First aid station.

1252. Путь свободен.
Road open.

1253. Рабочие на пути.
Men working.

1254. Район.
County.

1255. Ремонт дороги.
Road under repair.

1256. Сквозной проезд закрыт.
No thoroughfare.

1257. Скользко (в холодную) в дождливую
погоду.
Slippery (in cold) in rainy weather.

1258. Стоянка воспрещается.
Parking prohibited.

1259. Стоянка такси.
Taxi stand.

1260. Стой!
Stop!

1261. Справки.
Information.

1262. Справочное бюро.
Information bureau.

1263. Такси.
Taxi.

1264. Ток высокого напряжения.
High tension line.

1265. Только для легкового движения.
Passenger cars only.

1266. Только для грузового движения.
Trucks only.

1267. Трамвай.
Streetcar.

1268. Тунель.
Underground pass.

1269. Тупик.
Dead end.

1270. Уборная.
Toilet.

1271. Узкая дорога.
Narrow road.

1272. Улица.
Street.

1273. Через.
Via.

1274. Школа.
School.

1275. Школа — медленная езда.
School—drive slow.

1276. Шоссе.
Highway.

1277. Шоссейная дорога.
Paved road (highway).

APPENDIX VII (not recorded)
SIGNS AND PUBLIC NOTICES

1278. Ателье бытового обслуживания.
Valet service.

1279. Ателье индивидуального пошива.
Custom made clothing shop.

1280. Багажная квитанция.
Baggage check (receipt).

1281. Багажный вагон.
Luggage van.

1282. Бакалейная лавка.
Grocery store.

1283. Бакалея.
Groceries.

1284. Бар.
Bar.

1285. Берегись (автомобиля) поезда.
Beware of (automobile) train.

1286. Бесплатная стоянка.
Free parking.

1287. Библиотека.
Library.

1288. Биллиард.
Billiards.

1289. Больница.
Hospital.

1290. Ботанический сад.
Botanical garden.

1291. Бюро обслуживания туристов.
Tourist service bureau.

1292. Бюро приёма и распределения прибывающих.
Reception (at the hotel).

1293. Вагон-ресторан.
Dining car.

1294. Ванная.
Bathroom.

1295. Велосипедная езда запрещена.
Bicycles prohibited.

1296. Велосипеды.
Bicycles.

1297. Вина и спиртные напитки.
Wines and alcoholic beverages.

1298. Вниз.　　　　Вверх.
Downwards.　Upwards.

1299. Воздушная почта.
Air mail.

1300. Вокзал.
Railroad station.

1301. Вскакивать и соскакивать на ходу строго воспрещается.
Getting on or off while car is in motion is strictly prohibited.

1302. Вход.
Entrance, admission.

1303. Вход (воспрещается) воспрещен.
Entrance prohibited.

1304. Вход свободный.
Admission free.

1305. Выдача багажа.
Luggage room (incoming).

1306. Вывески.
Signs.

1307. Выход.
Exit.

1308. Выходной день.
Day off.

1309. Газетный киоск.
Newsstand.

1310. Галантерея.
Dry goods.

1311. Гардероб.
Overcoat check room.

1312. Гастроном.
Delicatessen.

1313. Гастрономический магазин.
Delicatessen.

1314. Глазной врач.
Oculist.

1315. Городская библиотека.
City library.

1316. Городской совет (горсовет).
City council.

1317. Горячая вода.
Hot water.

1318. Горячие сосиски.
Hot wieners.

1319. Гостиница.
Hotel.

1320. Государственная библиотека.
State library.

1321. Государственная художественная галлерея.
State art gallery.

1322. Государственный банк (госбанк).
State bank.

1323. Государственный универсальный магазин (ГУМ).
State department store (GUM).

1324. Грузовики.
Trucks.

1325. Дамская парикмахерская.
Ladies' hairdresser.

1326. Дата.
Date.

1327. Дворец пионеров.
Palace of pioneers.

1328. Дворец труда.
Palace of labor.

1329. Дворник.
Janitor.

1330. Действительно до . . .
Valid until . . .

1331. Депо.
Depot.

1332. Дирекция.
Administration.

1333. Для (велосипедистов) мотоциклистов.
For (bicycles) motorcycles.

1334. Для женщин.
For ladies.

1335. Для курящих.
For smokers.

1336. Для мужчин.
For men.

1337. Для некурящих.
Non-smoker.

1338. Для пассажиров первого класса.
For passengers of the first class.

1339. Дом культуры.
House of culture.

1340. Железнодорожные пути.
Railroad tracks.

1341. Железнодорожный раз'езд.
Railroad siding.

1342. Завод.
Plant.

1343. Заказные письма.
Registered letters.

1344. Закрыто.
Closed.

1345. Закрыто на каникулы.
Closed for vacation.

1346. Закрыто от . . . до . . .
Closed from . . . till . . .

1347. Закрыто по воскресеньям и праздникам.
Closed on Sundays and holidays.

1348. Закусочная.
Snack bar.

1349. Зал ождания.
Waiting room.

1350. Занимайте места согласно взятым блетам.
Take seats in accordance with your tickets.

1351. Занято.
Occupied.

1352. Запасной выход.
Emergency exit.

1353. Звонок.
Bell.

1354. Здесь купаться строго воспрещается.
Bathing here is strictly prohibited.

1355. Злые собаки.
Vicious dogs.

1356. Зоологический сад.
Zoological gardens.

1357. Зубной врач.
Dentist.

1358. Иностранная валюта.
Foreign money.

1359. Исполком.
Executive committee.

1360. Камера хранения ручного багажа.
Check room for hand baggage.

1361. Карета скорой помощи.
Ambulance.

1362. Касса.
Box office.

1363. Кассир.
Cashier.

1364. Кафе.
Coffee shop.

1365. Кафе-кондитерская.
Coffee and pastry shop.

1366. Квитанция.
Receipt.

1367. Кино.
Cinema.

1368. Кладбище.
Cemetery.

1369. Клуб.
Club.

1370. Книжный магазин.
Book store.

1371. Колхоз.
Collective farm.

1372. Кондитерская.
Confectioners.

1373. Кормить животных строго воспрещается.
Feeding the animals is prohibited.

1374. Косметический кабинет.
Beauty salon.

1375. Купаться воспрещается.
Bathing prohibited.

1376. Курить строго воспрещается.
Smoking strictly prohibited.

1377. Лестница.
Stairs.

1378. Лифт.
Elevator.

1379. Ловить рыбу с моста воспрещается.
Fishing from the bridge prohibited.

1380. Магазин дамских принадлежностей.
Ladies' clothing store.

1381. Магазин мужских принадлежностей.
Men's clothing store.

1382. Магазин шляп.
Milliners' *or* hatters'.

1383. Магазин юного натуралиста.
Pet shop.

1384. Марки.
Stamps.

1385. Мастерская индивидуальных пошивок.
Clothes made to order (shop for custom made clothing).

1386. Мебелированные комнаты.
Furnished rooms.

1387. Мебель.
Furniture.

1388. Мебельный магазин.
Furniture store.

1389. Медленная езда.
Drive slow.

1390. Междугородняя телефонная станция.
Long distance telephone operator.

1391. Мороженое.
Ice cream.

1392. Моссовет.
Moscow city council.

1393. Мотоциклы.
Motorcycles.

1394. Мужская парикмахерская.
Barbershop (men's).

1395. Мясная лавка.
Butcher.

1396. Наверх.
Upwards.

1397. На прокат.
For hire, rent.

1398. Не курить.
Do not smoke.

1399. Не плевать на пол.
Do not spit on the floor.

1400. Не сорить.
Do not litter.

1401. Не шуметь.
No noise.

1402. Носильщик.
Porter.

1403. Облисполком.
Oblast executive committee.

1404. Обмен иностранной валюты.
Foreign money exchange.

1405. Общежитие.
Dormitory.

1406. Окурки на пол не бросать.
Do not throw cigarette butts on the floor.

1407. Остановка автобуса.
Bus stop.

1408. Остановка трамвая.
Streetcar stop.

1409. Остерегайтесь карманных воров.
Beware of pickpockets.

1410. Осторожно.
Caution.

1411. Осторожно, окрашено.
Caution, fresh paint.

1412. Отбросы.
Refuse.

1413. Отделение (милиции).
Police (militia) precinct.

1414. Отель.
Hotel.

1415. Открыто.
Open.

1416. Открыто от . . . до . . .
Open from . . . till . . .

1417. Отход.
Departure.

1418. Парикмахерская.
Barbershop (ladies and men).

1419. Парк культуры и отдыха.
Park of culture and rest.

1420. Партком.
Party committee.

1421. Парфюмерия.   Парфюмерный магазин.
Perfume.   Cosmetic store.

1422. Пассажирский вокзал.
Passenger station.

1423. Пассажиры 1-го класса.
Passengers of the first class.

1424. Пассажиры 2-го класса.
Passengers of the second class.

1425. Пассажиры 3-го класса.
Passengers of the third class.

1426. Пекарня.
Bakery.

1427. Переводчик.
Interpreter.

1428. Переходите улицу только на перекрестке.
За нарушение штраф.
Cross the street at corners only. Fines for
violation.

1429. Переходите улицу по сигналу.
Cross the street on a signal.

1430. Перон.
Railroad platform.

1431. Перонный билет.
Platform ticket.

1432. Пешеходы.
Pedestrians.

1433. Пивная.
Beershop.

1434. Пиво распивочно и на вынос.
Beer, served at counter and to take out.

1435. Письма заграницу.
Letters for abroad (Foreign mail).

1436. Питьевая вода.
Drinking water.

1437. Подарки.
Gifts.

1438. Подпись.
Signature.

1439. Пожарный сигнал.
Fire alarm.

1440. Портниха.
Dressmaker.

1441. Портной.
Tailor.

1442. Посылки.
Parcel post.

1443. Почта и телеграф.
Post office and telegraph.

1444. Почтовый перевод.
Money order.

1445. Почтовый ящик.
Mail box.

1446. Похоронное бюро.
Funeral parlor.

1447. Прачечная.
Laundry.

1448. Прейскурант.
Price list.

1449. Прибытие поездов.
Arrival of trains.

1450. Прием багажа.
Luggage checked through.

1451. Продажа спиртных напитков воспрещается.
Sale of alcoholic beverages prohibited.

1452. Проезд закрыт.
No thoroughfare.

1453. Продовольственный магазин *or* продмаг
Grocery store.

1454. Просьба . . .
You are requested . . .

1455. Просьба соблюдать чистоту.
You are requested to keep the premises clean.

1456. Просят . . .
You are requested . . .

1457. Просят не говорить громко.
You are requested not to speak loud.

1458. Прохладительные напитки.
Cool drinks.

1459. Проход воспрещается.
No trespassing.

1460. Пульмановский вагон.
Sleeper (Pullman).

1461. Радио.
Radio.

1462. Райсовет.
Regional council.

1463. Расписание поездов.
Railroad timetable.

1464. Ремонт.
Repairs.

1465. Ремонтная мастерская.
Repair shop.

1466. Ресторан.
Restaurant.

1467. Сберегательная касса *or* сберкасса.
Savings bank.

1468. Свободно.
Free.

1469. Сдается в наем.
To let.

1470. Сегодня спектакля нет.
No performance today.

1471. Совхоз.
State farm.

1472. Сорить на улице строго воспрещается.
    Штраф три рубля.
Littering on the street is prohibited.
    Three rubles fine.

1473. Спальный вагон.
Sleeper.

1474. Спасательная лодка.
Life boat.

1475. Спасательный пояс.
Life preserver.

1476. Спектакль на сегодня отменён.
Performance for tonight cancelled.

1477. Спортивные принадлежности.
Sports goods.

1478. Справки.
Information.

1479. Справочное бюро.
Information bureau.

1480. Стоянка воспрещается.
Parking prohibited.

1481. Стоянка такси.
Taxi stand.

1482. Табачная лавка.
Tobacco shop.

1483. Телевидение.
Television.

1484. Телевизоры.
Television sets.

1485. Телефон.
Telephone.

1486. Товарный вокзал.
Freight station.

1487. Товары исключительной свежести.
Exceptionally fresh food products.

1488. Толкать от себя.
Push.

1489. Трамвай идёт в депо.
Streetcar going to the depot.

1490. Туалетные комнаты.
Toilets.

1491. Тянуть к себе.
Pull.

1492. Уборные.
Toilets.

1493. Университет.
University.

1494. Универсальный магазин *or* универмаг.
Department store.

1495. Уходя гасите свет.
Turn off the light when leaving.

1496. Фабрика.
Factory.

1497. Фотография.
Photographer's shop.

1498. Фруктовая лавка.
Fruit shop.

1499. Химическая чистка.
Dry cleaning.

1500. Хлебная лавка.
Bakery shop.

1501. Ходить и ездить по путям строго воспрещается.
Walking and driving on tracks is strictly prohibited.

1502. Ходить по траве строго воспрещается.
Keep off the grass.

1503. Цветочный магазин.
Flower shop.

1504. Цены по прейскуранту.
Firm prices.

1505. ЦК КПСС.
Central Committee of the Communist Party of the Soviet Union.

1506. Чистка сапог и ботинок.
Boot and shoe shine.

1507. Школа.
School.

1508. Штраф.
Fine.

1509. Экскурсии.
Excursions.

1510. Экскурсовод.
Excursion guide.

1511. Экспресс.
Express train.

1512. Электрические приборы.
Electric appliances.

1513. Яд! Не принимать внутрь.
Poison! Do not take internally.

APPENDIX VIII (not recorded)
PERSONAL LETTER

Simple personal letters and cards of greeting can be constructed from phrases and sentences in *Listen and Learn Russian*. The following model letter gives correct Russian letter form and sentences that can be adapted to similar situations. The English translation follows.

Москва
3. X—1958

Милый Коля!

Мы благополучно прибыли в Москву вчера рано утром и остановились в гостинице "Украина".

Когда наш поезд отошел от станции, мы с женой долго не ложились спать и говорили о наших впечатлениях от посещения Ленинграда и о всех наших новых друзьях, которые сделали наше пребывание там таким приятным.

Сегодня мы пойдем осматривать Кремль и старинные царские покои, а вечером собираемся на балет "Бахчисарайский фонтан"

в Большом Театре. Наше планы на ближай-
шие дни включают посещение Третьяковской
галлереи, музея Толстого, показательной
школы интерната, детских ясель, поездку по
Каналу Москва-Волга и футбольный матч на
знаменитом стадионе в Лужниках. Без сомне-
ния, мы увидим массу всего интересного и
получим большое удовольствие.

Как у вас дела? Что вы поделываете?
Как чувствует себя Лидия Алексеевна? Про-
шёл ли её насморк? Как поживает Борис
Владимирович и его жена? Как ваши отец и
мать? Пожалуйста кланяйтесь им от нас.

Ну, пора кончать. Жена торопит меня, так
как у нас на сегодня большая программа.
Она вам всем шлёт привет и лучшие поже-
лания.

Пожалуйста пишите нам, как вы обещали.
После первого августа наш адрес будет:

> СССР
> г. Севастополь
> ул. Пушкина, № 5, кв. 11

а после двадцатого августа пишите нам "до
востребования" на Американский Экспресс в
Риме.

Спасибо вам за все, что вы для нас сделали.
Пишите, не забывайте. Привет всем зна-
комым.

> Всего наилучшего.
> С приветом,
> Ваши,
> Мэри и Биль.

Moscow
Dear Kolya: October 3, 1958.

We arrived safely in Moscow yesterday early in the morning, and put up at the Hotel Ukraine.

After our train left the station, my wife and I stayed up late, and kept talking about the impressions of our visit to Leningrad, and about all our new friends who made our stay there so very pleasant.

Today we are going to do the Kremlin and the ancient chambers of the tsars, and in the evening we intend to see the ballet, "The Bakhchisaray Fountain". Our plans for the near future include a visit to the Tretyakov Gallery, to Tolstoy's Museum, to a model boarding school, a nursery, a trip along the Moskva-Volga Canal, and a soccer match at the famous stadium in Luzhniki. No doubt, we shall see many interesting things and have a good time.

How is everything with you? What have you been doing? How is Lydia Alekseevna feeling? Has she recovered from her cold? How are Boris Vladimirovich and his wife? How are your father and mother? Please remember us to them.

Well, it is time to close. My wife is urging me to hurry since we have such a vast program for today. She sends her greetings and best wishes to all of you.

Please write to us as you have promised. After the first of August our address will be:

USSR
Sevastopol
Pushkin Street, No 5, apt. 11

but after August 20, better write to us care of American Express in Rome.

Thank you for everything you have done for us. Write, and do not forget. Greetings to all our acquaintances.

Best of everything.
Greetings,
Yours,
Mary and Bill.

INDEX

All the sentences, words, and phrases in this book are numbered consecutively from 1 to 1513. The entries in this index refer to these numbers. In addition, each major section heading (capitalized) is indexed according to page number **in bold face.** Parts of speech are indicated by the following italic abbreviations: *adj.* for adjective, *adv.* for adverb, *n.* for noun, and *v.* for verb.